Hypnosis

Understanding How It Can Work for You

Sean F. Kelly, Ph.D.
Reid J. Kelly, ACSW

A Merloyd Lawrence Book

Addison-Wesley Publishing Company, Inc.
Reading, Massachusetts Menlo Park, California
Don Mills, Ontario Wokingham, England Amsterdam
Sydney Singapore Tokyo Mexico City Bogotá
Santiago San Juan

Library of Congress Cataloging in Publication Data
Kelly, Sean F.
   Hypnosis, understanding how it can work for you.

   "A Merloyd Lawrence book."
   Bibliography: p.
   Includes index.
   1. Hypnotism – Therapeutic use. I. Kelly, Reid J.
II. Title.
RC495.K45 1985   615.8'512   84–24299
ISBN 0–201–15255–X
ISBN 0–201–15256–8 (hard)

Cover design by Marshall Henrichs
Text design by Douglass Scott
Set in 12-point Galliard by DEKR Corporation
ISBN 0–201–15255–X
ISBN 0–201–15256–8 (hard)
ABCDEFG–DO–898765
First Printing, February 1985

This book is dedicated to Amy and Ian.

Contents

NOTE TO THE READER

This book is intended as an introduction – for patients, health professionals, psychotherapists, and teachers – to the growing field of clinical hypnosis. The uses, techniques, and concepts are therefore only broadly sketched. The serious student who wishes to pursue the intricacies, nuances of theory and opinion, and details of the science is referred to the bibliography, which can serve as a guided entrée into the scientific literature.

In the case examples we have recorded mostly successes. Obviously, hypnosis does not cure everyone or everything. It is a powerful but not omnipotent technique. When hypnosis does not work, it is generally because some other influential factor is at play. When the resistance to change is too great, it must be dealt with in the same manner as any resistance in psychotherapy, an effort which is beyond the scope of this book. In the case examples we have tried to make clear when the techniques are useful alone and when hypnosis should be considered as an adjunct to psychotherapy.

Part I
The Nature of Hypnosis

All sciences alike have descended from magic and superstition, but none has been so slow as hypnosis in shaking off the evil associations of its origins.

Clark Hull, 1933

I
Myth and Reality

POPULAR MYTHS AND MISPERCEPTIONS
AND THEIR SOURCES

Hypnosis – the word summons a number of stereotyped images and associations: a gold pocket watch swinging from a chain, an ominously soothing voice intoning, "Look deep into my eyes," sleepiness, dwindling willpower, faulty self-control, amnesia, a flood of vivid memories, an unleashing of primordial impulses, mindless obedience, reincarnation, Dracula . . . magic.

The notion of hypnosis is clouded by myth and misunderstanding. Perhaps the most pervasive and frightening fiction about hypnosis is that, for better or for worse (and it is usually worse), one is under the complete and utter control of the hypnotist. In *The Cabinet of Doctor Caligari,* the doctor hypnotizes a man who thus becomes his zombielike slave. Caligari keeps the unfortunate fellow locked up in a box during the day, sending him out in the dark hours, programmed to commit murder. Similarly, Dracula needs only to fix his red-eyed gaze on his victims to sap them of their will to resist.

Hypnosis has received further sensational publicity

3

and notoriety through its misleading but tenacious association with reincarnation. Believers, perhaps the most famous of them being Brydie Murphy, state that it is possible, in trance, to experience memories from previous lifetimes. They back their beliefs by pointing out that when hypnotized, people suddenly develop a previously nonexistent ability to speak a foreign language or accurately describe ancient civilizations.

In fantasy only does hypnosis ensure transcendence of normal mental and physical capabilities. Thus the fictional Svengali can take the equally fictional tone-deaf Trilby and, through hypnotic suggestions, turn her into a singer of unparalleled ability.

Hypnosis is widely and wrongly presumed both to render the subject incapable of lying and to rob him of the ability to keep embarrassing secrets confidential. Those who so believe tend to perceive a hypnotist as having more than human status, as being an all-powerful clairvoyant. Claims, most often overblown but sometimes accurate, that hypnosis prevents branding irons from burning, causes blisters to rise on command, and increases breast size smack of tawdry theatricality.

Our understanding of the phenomenon behind hypnosis is distorted by its vogue in night club acts where volunteers ostensibly experience age regressions, perform impressive physical feats, or make utter fools of themselves. Members of the audience suddenly discover they cannot leave their seats because they are bound by imaginary glue. Volunteers hold themselves rigidly suspended between two chairs like "human planks." On cue, a participant follows a "posthypnotic suggestion" to jump on

4

a table and shout, "The British are coming!" The stage hypnotist is supposed to have the "power" to make volunteers do whatever he bids.

Thanks to fiction and theatrical demonstrations, "hypnosis" has become a commonly used and familiar term. When Woody Woodpecker wiggles his fingers and magnetic waves come forth, even children know the bird is practicing hypnotism. Yet this supposedly well-known, familiar term is in fact one of the most generally misunderstood and misused words in the field of psychology. Much of what is called "hypnotism" has little or nothing to do with the true event.

Nor is the confusion about hypnosis confined to members of a lay audience. Even those supposedly well versed in the practical application of psychology are not always clear as to what hypnosis is or what it can and cannot do. For example, a psychiatrist had been treating an extremely shy man in psychoanalytic psychotherapy. For a number of years they had talked about the origins of the patient's fear of women, all without much progress in the patient's social life. When the doctor began attending a workshop on hypnotic techniques, he became excited and eager to test out his new skills on his patient. At the earliest possible moment, the psychiatrist hypnotized his patient, suggesting that he relax and imagine asking a woman out to dinner. He further suggested that the patient would do in real life what he had practiced during trance. The results were fantastic. The patient returned a week later to report that he had asked a woman out and that she had accepted. The couple had enjoyed themselves so much that a second evening was planned. The psychiatrist, flushed with success, reported his wonderful achievement to his workshop leader and added his testimonial to the efficacy of hypnosis. His teacher congratulated him, but then threw a bucket of cold water on the burning enthusiast: had he ever tried telling the patient to ask a woman out on a date, without using hypnosis? Indignantly, the psychiatrist replied, "Of course not! It would be very unpsychoanalytic to tell a patient what to do outside of hypnosis."

The ritual of hypnosis allowed the doctor to give direct, sensible suggestions, an approach that was not included in his usual therapeutic repertoire. To the extent that this directive technique was extraordinary, and to the extent that it worked wonders, "hypnosis" itself became a force that the doctor found special and wonderful.

Had he understood the hypnotic process better (to say nothing of analytic theory and practice), its mystique might have vanished and it would have seemed less impressive. Events that are not well understood have a way of appearing miraculous, even magical.

It is perhaps the universal and deeply rooted human wish for and fear of magic that does the most to enhance and perpetuate the myths surrounding hypnosis. It is as human to retain some childhood wish for a benevolent being who can easily cure any ill, erase any anxiety, or make it simple to control a bad habit or an unacceptable urge as it is to harbor some childhood fear of a malevolent figure who cannot be opposed or denied, no matter how evil.

A hypnotist of questionable scruples or training tries to play on this facet of human nature. For him an aura

6

of magic and mystique is vital. He depends on exciting trappings and on maintaining the illusion of irresistible "power." Rather than dispel the common misperceptions about hypnosis, he encourages them.

Important also in perpetuating the myth of the powerful hypnotist is the very human desire to be rid of everyday inhibitions. People do, for instance, wish sometimes to be the center of attention or to escape from their own repressive prohibitions. A stage hypnotist offers license to their free expression by "taking responsibility" for them. If an entertainer can get a volunteer to experience even the slightest alteration in perception, the subject assumes that the hypnotist *made* it happen. One can point to hypnosis as the culprit responsible for any unacceptable behavior, in much the same way as one can say, "It was the drink talking, not me."

The entertainer begins his act with a bit of smooth patter designed to catch and focus the audience's attention. Then he gives simple, indirect, subtle, or disguised suggestions to his audience and watches to see who responds to them. He might state that a hypnotized person will feel his or her arm become light enough to float up in the air. A shrewd performer will recognize that those of the assembly who then lift their arms, if only to scratch their heads, rest their chins, or shift position, are demonstrating a potential for suggestibility.

The stage hypnotist selects his volunteers only from this group of responsive subjects. Of this number, those who agree to come up on stage are, by the very nature of their willingness to participate, indicating a desirable streak of exhibitionism.

7

These participants are then exposed to some sort of hypnotic induction and to a continuous, not so subtle bit of social pressure. Volunteers who initially get the limelight but then prove to be too inhibited either to allow a trance or to be very entertaining are asked to sit down. They are not excused with a gentle thank-you, however. They are mocked, ridiculed, or tied in logical knots by the clever performer. There is intense social pressure to do as the stage hypnotist wishes, and for the remaining volunteers the choice is quite clear. They can buck the system by refusing to comply with the entertainer's suggestions, thus retaining their dignity and self-control, but having to endure public humiliation. Or they can participate as the hypnotist desires, with the rationale that no matter what they do, the hypnotist is responsible.

For those who choose to participate, the entertainer goes through a stereotypic, theatrical hypnotic induction which may (but does not necessarily) result in a trance. The volunteers who do in fact experience the slightly altered perception that often accompanies a mild trance will tend to reason that this alteration happened because the stage hypnotist said it would. If he could produce one such phenomenon, then he must cause subsequent ones as well. The perception is that the hypnotist's commands are irresistible. The reality is that a willing subject was motivated to allow himself to become hypnotized and/or to transfer some degree of responsibility to the hypnotist.

Nothing that is required of members of this kind of audience is anything that, given the proper motivation, they could or would not have done without hypnosis.

Thus, the onstage volunteers who do not become hypnotized can perform just as well as their hypnotized counterparts. The "human plank" feat, for instance, looks spectacular but can easily be done outside of hypnosis. Because the feat is demonstrated after a hypnotic induction, however, the illusion is that hypnosis caused it.

A famous professor used to appear in college psychology classes to lecture on hypnosis. After he was introduced, he would give his students a variety of unusual tasks: to take off their shoes, to wear someone else's hat, to stand on a chair, and so on. Once they had complied with these instructions, the teacher would point out what odd things they had done. He would then emphasize that if the students had first been hypnotized and then given such tasks, they would have assumed that it was hypnosis which made them act strangely. It was the professor's prestige and authority, not his hypnotic ability, that assured him of their compliance.

Doctors, lawyers, and experimenters, like professors, hold positions in which they may expect some degree of obedience. A student can test this point easily. Pick out two casual acquaintances. Go up to the first and say, "Do ten push-ups, please." The most probable response is, "Why should I?" Then go to the second and say, "I'm conducting an experiment for my class. I need to see how long it takes you to do ten push-ups. Please start now." The likely response is ten quick push-ups.

Because defining a situation as an experiment (or therapy session, class hour, legal matter, medical exam, etc.) gives the experimenter (or therapist, professor, lawyer, doctor, etc.) a great deal of control over the participant, it is impossible to assess with any accuracy to what degree hypnosis increases that control.

While hypnosis, in and of itself, does not guarantee obedience, it has been correlated with an enhancement of certain other traits and responses. For instance, hypnosis is associated with an improvement in the ability to remember. This proven relationship, however, when intertwined with half-truths, distorted, or selectively emphasized, has been used to back up some dubious claims. The theory of reincarnation, for example, relies heavily on the proven association of memory skills with hypnosis. What the theory does not take into account is that hypnosis also enhances the ability to imagine.

The request "Tell me about your prior life" is not necessarily only and always a command to conjure up memories of early life (or, as some theories would have it, an earlier lifetime). It is as well a cue to imagine. It is important to realize that people are, in fact, equally adept at describing the future as the past. When told to envision the year 2300, a hypnotized subject can render a beautifully embellished account of the upcoming century with just as much confidence and conviction as he or she can describe ancient Egypt.

Instead of concluding from such reports that this particular subject once really lived with the ancient pharaohs or mentally time-warped himself into the future, one might rather understand such descriptions as the result of a rich mixture of imagination and previously forgotten factual data.

For instance, one can ask a very responsive subject what life would be like in Elizabethan England, in the

Macedonian army of Alexander, or in a Neanderthal cave. When hypnotized, he or she will often produce vivid and accurately detailed descriptions. These well-embroidered accounts often come as a surprise to the person providing them, who will claim no previous conscious awareness of the facts just stated.

Although there have been some people who willingly participate in fraudulent hypnotic schemes, a large number voice their disclaimers in good faith. But in most cases the uncanny descriptions elicited through hypnosis can be dated back to childhood remembrances. Memories of foreign-speaking nannies, childhood storybooks, or performances have simply been consciously forgotten. Hypnosis allows access to the pertinent information in these lost recollections.

THE REALITY OF HYPNOSIS

Contrary to popular opinion, the real event of hypnosis is not dramatic, nor is it remarkably different from other, more familiar states of mind. Many subjects whom experts would consider very responsive have an interesting reaction to their first hypnotic experience. At the conclusion of the trance, they open their eyes and say something like, "That was very relaxing and pleasant, Doctor, but I wasn't hypnotized." These subjects may be skeptical, citing reasons such as "I knew what was going on"; "I remember everything"; "I felt in control"; "I felt I could stop it at any time"; "I've felt this way before when I was not hypnotized."

These observations reflect some of the usual misunderstandings and preconceived notions about hypnosis. Also reflected, however, is the difficulty of describing any state of consciousness. It is as hard to define accurately the subjective experience of "awake," "alert," "relaxed," and "daydreaming," as it is to define "hypnotized." At best such descriptions are approached by metaphor and simile, by successive approximations and negative definitions.

As a broad term, "hypnosis" can be used and understood to encompass a variety of meanings, some more accurate than others. A correct, though incomplete, definition of hypnosis is that state of consciousness which occurs in the setting of willing participation in a hypnotic induction.

A hypnoidal state is a form of hypnosis that occurs commonly and spontaneously in everyday life. Many people routinely lapse into such a state, never considering it anything less than normal. For instance, you are driving in a car along a familiar route, perhaps home from work. On arrival, you think, "I don't remember passing the shopping mall." Now, the actual disappearance of the mall would most certainly have caught your attention. It must have been, then, that you were in that common state of "automatic pilot" which allows you to drive along, letting a fraction of the mind's attention do the driving while the rest wanders off. At times, this "highway hypnosis" becomes so severe as to produce accidents:

> *You look up at the highway and it is straight for miles, coming at you, with the black line down the center coming at and at you, black and slick and tarry-shining*

against the white of the slab, and the heat dazzles up
from the white slab so that only the black line is clear,
coming at you with the whine of the tires, and if you
don't quit staring at that line and don't take a few deep
breaths and slap yourself hard on the back of the neck
you'll hypnotize yourself and you'll come to just at the
moment when the right front wheel hooks over into the
black dirt shoulder off the slab. . . .

Robert Penn Warren
All the King's Men

More benign, hypnoticlike phenomena routinely happen not only in everyday life, but also in the contexts of Transcendental Meditation, repetitive prayer, and the "Relaxation Response."

The major, shared element of both such hypnoidal and more formal hypnotic experiences is the alteration of perception or awareness. An example of this kind of change can easily be demonstrated and experienced. The reader might want to try the following simple suggestions as an experiment.

Sit up straight and make yourself comfortable. Close your eyes and relax. While in this position, begin to think about how it would feel to let your head fall forward. Think of it in a variety of ways. Develop a mental image of how it would look if your head were to droop forward. Imagine how it would feel to have your head swaying back and forth, more and more forward. Feel your neck become tired, the muscles becoming limp. Feel the drooping, swaying, heaviness of your head. Soon your chin will be resting on your chest. Open your eyes now.

13

The important element in this even is not what occurred, but how it occurred. You know that your head,
in reality, did not suddenly gain ten pounds, your spine
didn't jellify, nor did your muscles go on vacation. Nevertheless, you heard the suggestions that your head would
go down, and soon it rested comfortably on your chest.

Clearly, one could prevent a change in position of
the head by refusing to participate, to lend one's imagination to this experiment. Moreover, one could hold
one's head erect, resisting any urge to move it. Finally,
one could drop or push one's chin to the chest, making
the movement a consciously controlled decision. Choosing to lower the head differs from letting oneself respond
to the suggestion. In hypnotic suggestion, the usual motor control functions are not engaged to move the head,
nor are they putting on the brakes to hold it in place.
Rather, the motor controls seem to be in neutral, neither
producing nor preventing motion. Imagination then
grows more and more important.

A spectator at a sports match will often make ges-
tures and movements which are, in fact, recognizable as
minute, inhibited versions of the athletes' motions. Neither deliberately preventing nor intending to make these
movements, the spectator becomes so identified with the
athlete that he vividly imagines he is doing what the
athlete is doing. In a small way, the spectator turns his
mental image into muscular reality.

This transition from mind to muscle may sometimes
be seen at baby showers. The guests tie a piece of ribbon
to the pregnant woman's wedding ring and hold it suspended over her belly. The direction of the swing is

supposed to predict the baby's sex. The ring prediction is, of course, a reflection of what the holder believes, hopes, or imagines the baby to be. Such a practice and the popular myth of using a gold pocket watch to induce hypnosis probably share a common ancestor: the Chevral pendulum. This device was originally designed not to mesmerize a subject but to measure responses to suggestions heard in an "awake" state. Furthermore, it was the subject, not the hypnotist, who held the pendulum.

You can easily make your own swinging device. All you need is a long, flexible piece of chain or string and a weight. A ring on a ribbon, a locket on a necklace, a watch on a chain, or some keys on a piece of twine will work equally well.

Hold the unweighted end between the thumb and middle finger, bending the wrist. Place your elbow on a chair arm or the corner of a table, with your arm nearly vertical. Let the chain and weight hang straight down, unimpeded. Hold them still, without any sway. Now think about the possibility of the weight beginning to swing. Think of it swinging in a clockwise circle, and visualize it circling. It will probably begin to do so. Then imagine it swinging back and forth before you. It will. Next, imagine it changing to a counterclockwise circle. Finally, let it swing straight toward and away from you.

Success in moving the weight in the imagined directions does not depend on telekinesis or any other mystical phenomena. Your fingers make the fantasied motions to an imperceptible degree. The pendulum, however, acts like a fulcrum and lever to magnify the angle of the arc to the point where it is clearly visible in the movement of the weight. In the instances of the head falling forward, the sports spectator's motions, and the wedding ring trick, thinking or imagining a movement produces a tendency to make that same movement. This type of event is integral to hypnosis.

The quality that permits such imagined motions to be executed in fact, and that is most important in distinguishing the essence of hypnosis, is a trait labeled "primary suggestibility." This hallmark of hypnosis occurs in the context of voluntary participation in the distortion of experience. Two definitions can be applied to it: (1) the performance of movements as a result of the strong, perhaps repeated suggestion that they will occur (e.g., one's head falls forward, the Chevral pendulum moves), and/or (2) the experience of cognitive or perceptual changes as a result of firm, often repetitive suggestions that such alterations will occur (e.g., one's head *feels* heavy).

Primary suggestibility is a facet of personality that in turn can be broken down into various capacities. The ability to become absorbed is one such capacity. A person who demonstrates this ability is able to become so engrossed and narrowly focused on reading, listening to music, or watching a drama, for instance, that he or she becomes oblivious to the surroundings. With a narrowing of the perceptual field, the person can concentrate more intently on a chosen activity.

Marie Curie, as a child, was said to become so absorbed in a book that nothing could make her attention wander. As she sat, engrossed in her reading, her brothers and sisters would pile great mounds of toys around her.

16

Although completely walled in by playthings, Marie would not notice anything amiss until she was finished reading. Such a capacity is integral to primary suggestibility but would not by itself be enough to account for hypnotizability. The other essential component of this experience is an ability to dissociate partially from reality and at the same time to accept a secondary reality.

Having an imaginary playmate as a child, for instance, indicates a capacity for vivid imagination and intentional distortion of reality. The child knows his friend is not actually there as another human being, yet he will insist that a grownup move because the adult is sitting on and squashing his friend. The child can maintain simultaneous connectedness with actual reality and with the secondary, imaginative reality he has superimposed on it. He knows there is a difference between these two realities, yet he likes things this way, and he chooses to accept, ignore, or tolerate any resulting incongruities.

Both the abilities to imagine in this fashion and to become involved and absorbed in a pursuit are not only essential to hypnosis, but are integral to the enjoyment of the arts and to that state of mind found often in well-entertained audiences: the willing suspension of disbelief.

This common and enjoyable experience is subjectively similar to (although different in theory from) the experience of hypnosis. Just as one would not say that a theatergoer who happily immerses himself in the premises of the drama is therefore unable to distinguish between fantasy and reality, it is equally false to make such an assumption about someone who is hypnotized.

For instance, advertisements for *Superman: The*

Movie proclaimed, "You will believe a man can fly." No one much over the age of six left the movie believing that the actor Christopher Reeve had suddenly developed the ability to fly. Instead, as the ads indicated, it was hoped that the story would be compelling enough and the movie technically good enough that a viewer might easily ignore what he actually knew: people don't fly; he was in a theater, watching a movie projector show pictures of people acting. Such a moviegoer would prefer to ignore these realities and enjoy the show. He chooses to indulge himself in make-believe and immerse himself in the perceived fantasy. If a fire were to break out, however, not even the most engrossed members of the audience would wait for Superman to fly in and whisk them to safety.

The decision to participate in the premises of a drama, to give free play to the imagination, is something that, once chosen, can be revoked at any time. Such a decision is an active, ongoing, renewable process of willing to believe what is known to be fantasy. It is as though an alert, observant part of the brain were continually monitoring the situation and quietly deciding that it is all right to allow the part of the brain engaged in imagining to do so freely.

The hypnotized person knows what is going on, where and who he is, and that he is involved in a trance. Again, like the moviegoer, he has chosen to ignore and to hold in abeyance his usual logical, reality-orienting faculties. In a sense, a hypnotist involved in the hypnotic process acts like the part of the brain that permits the other to imagine. The hypnotist takes over as guardian and monitor of the critical faculties that the subject usually controls himself and thus becomes the interpreter of reality for the duration of the trance.

Consider the suggestion, common to many a hypnotic experience, that one's arm will feel heavy. Ordinarily, if you want to know how heavy your arm is, in effect you ask, "How heavy are you, arm?" Arm sends a message to the brain, "I am thus and so heavy." In hypnosis, however the subject ignores this source of data and relies on the hypnotist's interpretations of and statements about experience. If the hypnotist suggests, "Your arm is very heavy," the brain doesn't ask the arm how much it weighs. Instead, the brain sends a message to the arm, "You are very heavy, aren't you, arm?" Arm replies, "I sure am, just the way you told me I was." The direction of the flow of information is reversed in hypnosis.

The suggestion "Your arm is very heavy" does not immediately and automatically make the subject's arm very heavy. There is an important intermediate step. The subject hears the hypnotic suggestion, and, implicitly or explicitly, chooses to participate and to produce the suggested effect. The subject then sends the signal to his arm that it will feel heavy.

A person experiencing hypnosis can choose to dissociate himself not only from ordinary physical sensations but also from other internal sources of information. For example, each of us has an internal clock that gives us a temporal orientation. We know the present instant is "now" and can distinguish among present, past, and future. We can, furthermore, place these times in relation to both standard, external measures of time (time of day,

day of the week, season, and date) and milestones of time ("when I was twenty-three," "after the grandchildren were born," "when I first started working here").

In hypnosis, a subject might choose to deal with such an internal orientation in much the same way as he could deal with the weight of his arm. That is, rather than consult his internal clock for temporal orientation, he chooses to rely on the hypnotist's interpretation of time.

The hypnotist might, for instance, suggest, "It is no longer the present. You are going back into the past. It is now three years ago." The subject who accepts this suggestion then, in effect, says to himself, "I will not look at my internal clock. Instead, I will depend on the cues given to me to set up an imagined 'reality' for time."

The subject, while deciding to accept the hypnotist's time statement, ignores, but nevertheless remains aware of, the existence of his usual time sense. This internal time sense is available as an anchor or reference point from which he can calculate "three years ago."

Consider the inherent contradiction in the statement "It is now three years ago." This says "the present is the past," that "now" is "not now." As was the case with the heavy arm, the subject hears the hypnotist's suggestion, accepts this statement, including its contradiction (this is known as "trance logic"), and then produces the effect by telling himself that "now" is truly "not now."

This sequence demonstrates once again that hypnosis and all its effects have self-hypnosis at the core. It is the subject, really, who decides and determines the course of hypnosis and whether or not to translate the suggestions into actual experience. The observing part of the brain, the "voice" inside the subject's head, acts like an internal hypnotist and passes on the suggestions. After forming an alliance with an outside hypnotist, this fraction of the psyche carries out the job, becoming the hypnotist.

All hypnosis is self-hypnosis. The subject of an experiment in hypnosis, the volunteer participant in a night club, or the patient on the therapist's couch all give their consent, whether consciously or unconsciously, to become hypnotized. Alone or in the company of a hypnotist who serves as coach or guide, an individual decides to enter a state of enhanced imagination and concentration. This process is hypnosis.

2
Hypnotic Inductions

Hypnotic encounters vary widely from one another in accordance with differences in hypnotists' styles and subjects' personalities. Each experience is unique, never reoccurring in exactly the same way twice. What all do have in common, however, is an induction.

An induction is the process of focusing and enhancing concentration and imagination in such a way that the net result is the state of consciousness called hypnosis. The subject must become so involved in this process that he directs his attention away from the usual sources of orienting information, giving heed instead to the voice of the hypnotist.

Dim lights, quiet surroundings, comfortable seating, and serene tranquillity are *not* absolute requirements for induction of hypnosis. One can practice self-hypnosis on a commuter subway as easily as one can read a book there. However, since hypnosis involves concentration, it is most easily learned in a nondistracting setting where extraneous stimuli are minimal.

When, for instance, a person enters a sensory-deprivation tank, almost all perception is eliminated and the mind is deprived of its orienting information. If a voice is presented to the person in the tank, it tends to be seized upon and accepted because no other information contradicts it. Similarly, response to suggestion is enhanced in cases where the environment provides few cues. This has been demonstrated by research in the Antarctic. Although hypnotic inductions usually take place in less extreme settings, most involve closing the eyes. The rationale behind this procedure is that eye closure eliminates a great deal of orienting, and thus distracting, information.

Inductions may be formal or idiosyncratic, long or brief. Lengthy, detailed, and complicated induction methods are generally used when a subject is first learning to be hypnotized. Such complex inductions not only become unneccessary as experience with the hypnotic state grows, but are cumbersome.

As with any skill, early learning differs from finely honed ability. A reader of this book does not sound out each letter to get a word but reads several words at a time. Early hypnotic inductions, like early phonics, are the first steps. Later, the process is much swifter and things seem to come naturally.

To shift the metaphor, if the state of hypnosis is thought of as a "place" in the mind, first inductions are intended to teach you how to get there and to recognize that as the place called "hypnosis." The initial route taken is a rather sure and common one, which sticks to clearly marked main roads. As you become more adept and familiar with your destination, you can take shortcuts.

A patient once came to a session reporting that she was practicing her hypnotic exercises regularly, and added, "I've changed something – I hope that's all right.

I don't do the induction the way you taught me. Instead, I just sit down, close my eyes, and let my mind fall in on itself."

Now, this letting the mind "fall in on itself," as an entrée to hypnosis, makes perfect sense to many good, experienced subjects. However, telling a novice "Let your mind fall in on itself," is like telling a kindergarten child, "Just pick up the encyclopedia and read it."

For a novice's first four or five sessions, many therapists select a different induction from among the number of known formal methods. Using various techniques in this way teaches, in practical terms, that there is no single "correct ritual" involved in becoming hypnotized. The use of alternative methods helps to distinguish the essence of hypnosis from artifact. When a sense of experimentation is encouraged, the patient can try different ways and see which elements of each are the most comfortable and natural. Having arrived at the most satisfactory method, a patient can continue to use it in any further sessions.

Basic inductions may be cut, spliced, and broadened in a variety of ways. Examples follow below. After the first example, only those portions that are unique to each method are included. All contain greatly condensed versions of what a hypnotist might say to a subject.

Basic Induction Method

Sit comfortably and firmly in a relaxed position, with both your feet flat on the floor and your arms on the arms of the chair. Close your eyes: take a deep breath; hold it

*. . . let it out, and feel a sense of relaxation coming in as
the air is expelled. Nothing harmful will happen to you;
you will be safe. Just let whatever you find happening
happen, even if it is not what you expected. Just let it occur. Listen and concentrate on my voice and all that I
describe.*

The goal in this portion of the induction is to focus
attention and minimize extraneous stimuli, both external
(other sounds, sights), and internal (e.g., anxiety over a
new experience).

Since relaxation and anxiety are mutually exclusive,
a relaxed patient can't be distracted by anxiety. Thus
suggestions to minimize tension are often incorporated
into an induction.

*Feel yourself slowing down. Picture a still, calm pool or
pond. Picture a drop of water falling into the pond. As it
strikes the placid surface, it sends out ripples. As the first
ripple spreads, a second forms within it, then a third.
You see ripples within ripples within ripples, a series of
concentric rings.*

*Feel the ripples of relaxation spreading out from
your eyes across the muscles of your forehead, cheeks, and
jaws. Feel the spreading waves of relaxation in your
neck, your shoulders, your back, your chest, your stomach, your legs, your arms. Let it spread to reach the ends
of your toes and the tips of your fingers.*

Relaxation is not equivalent to hypnosis, nor is it
mandatory in an induction. However, it is so useful as a

treatment technique, both in and out of hypnosis, that it is often included in the induction process.

Imagine yourself floating, drifting, gliding. Perhaps you might imagine yourself on a raft, peacefully drifting on a gentle current. Or perhaps you might feel yourself become so light that you could float through the air like a bit of fluff, wafted along by a gentle breeze.

The hypnotist's version of reality comes to the fore as a sense of dissociation from usual reality increases. Trance logic is introduced, the patient being told that "here" is really on a "raft." The ability to "move" in this fashion from an imagined tension-provoking situation to one that is safe and relaxing becomes an important skill useful in any subsequent treatment sessions.

Notice your left hand. Feel the sensations—whether it is warm or cool, moist or dry. Think of the muscles in your hand, and you will find that they begin to twitch ever so slightly. Your hand and arm are becoming light. Now picture a large red helium balloon attached to your wrist, lifting it up, pulling at it ever so gently.

The balloon is lifting your arm up. Let your arm float up, just let your arm drift up with the balloon. That's right. Your arm feels so light that even if you tried, you could not lower your hand. Just try lowering your hand. You see, it stayed up. Right now it is too difficult for you to lower it.

Given here are two simple suggestions designed (1) to demonstrate to the subject that something special is occurring, and (2) to give the hypnotist a sense of how the subject is responding.

> *Now that you are familiar with the relaxed state of enhanced concentration and imagination known as hypnosis, it will be easier and easier to enter more and more quickly this state whenever you might wish to do so in the future.*

The ability to enter hypnosis quickly leaves more time for its actual *use*.

> *I am going to count backward from three, and at "one" you will open your eyes and be fully alert, feeling relaxed and refreshed, and your usual sensations and control will have returned. Now, "three," take a deep breath. "Two," let it out. "One!" Fully alert. How do you feel?*

The purpose of this last portion is to bring reality as defined by the hypnotist and regular reality together so that they are the same. The question at the end is phrased "How do you feel?" rather than "You feel fine" to emphasize that the subject is once again in charge of his experience.

Induction by Visual Fixation (The Braid Technique)

In this method, a thumbtack or a colored spot is placed on the wall opposite the subject's chair, somewhat above eye level. After the subject is seated, the hypnotist points out the spot or tack and calls it "the target." (Variations include the subject's hand, the opposite wall, or a spot on the ceiling.)

> *I would like you to look at that target, stare at the target. Focus all your attention on looking at that target and listening to my voice. If your eyes should wander, that's all right. Just bring them back to the target, just as if your mind should wander, just bring it back to my voice.*
>
> *As you stare at the target, you're going to begin to notice something a little unusual about this target. As you watch the target, it will begin to play tricks for you. Perhaps the edges will become blurred, or else very sharp and clear, as it goes in and out of focus. Perhaps it will seem to move about. It may even change color. As you stare, it may seem as though the target is not real, but rather perhaps superimposed on the background, like a picture taped onto it. The target may seem ringed by a halo of light. Whatever you see is fine. Just stare, focus, and concentrate.*

The hypnotist takes advantage of known physiological events, the changes mentioned, by predicting they will occur. Once the accuracy of his predictions is established, those that follow in the form of suggestions are expected to happen as well.

> *As you continue to stare, however, your eyes are beginning to feel very heavy, heavy and tired, like lead. Soon they will want to close of themselves. So heavy and tired. Your eyes feel hot and strained, more and more tired.*

They are beginning to blink more and more. It becomes harder and harder to stay open, until at last they close of themselves.

Often the hypnotist proceeds from this point into relaxation. However, the suggestions to relax could as well be done before the eyes are closed.

Arm-Lowering Method

Sit comfortably, and hold your right arm up with your hand at eye level, about a foot in front of you. I'd like you to pick out a spot on your hand, any spot at all, and I'm going to call that spot "the target."

The hypnotist continues as with the Braid method, then adds:

That hand is becoming very heavy, as though a lead weight were attached to it, pulling it down, more and more down, heavier and heavier. As that arm is pulled down, your eyelids become heavy.

Note the sense of dissociation/distance from the body that is subtly suggested by the reference to "that hand" rather than "your hand."

Sunset

Sit comfortably; close your eyes, and visualize a sunset. See the orb of the sun dropping below the horizon; watch as the color of the sky changes from sky blue to gold and red, to violet and black. Day is done. It is time to relax.

Sometimes the sense of dissociation is enhanced by having the subject imagine watching the sunset from the deck of an anchored boat. Imagining the sway of the boat can bring on a floating feeling.

Lungs Pumping Out Tension

This method is used for subjects who have experienced another hypnotic induction successfully.

> *Close your eyes; get yourself nicely relaxed; take a deep breath. Hold it, hold it . . . now breathe it out, and as you do, feel yourself become even more relaxed. Breathe slowly, regularly, and comfortably. As you do, you feel how with each breath you exhale you become ever more relaxed, as though your lungs were pumps, pumping all the tension out of your body. Imagine tension as a heavy, thick liquid, and it is being pumped out, leaving your body light, relaxed, and free of tension.*

Sometimes this imagery is incorporated into another induction as its relaxation portion, and sometimes it is used alone.

> *When your lungs have finished pumping out all the tension, you will be hypnotized.*

Draining Tension

Like the "Lungs Pumping" induction, this method serves either as an induction for the experienced or the relaxation portion of an induction.

As you settle into the chair, feel yourself relaxing, sink-ing down into the chair; let it hold you. Feel the chair as very strong; let it hold and support you. Feel yourself heavy and limp, like a warm, wet bath towel just dropped into the chair. As you feel so comfortably sunken into the chair, imagine openings in your feet and arms, openings out of which tension can drain. Feel the tension drain out of you. If any should start to build up in your body, it will again quickly run out.

Eye Roll

This method has its roots in an observation that en-tranced mystics are often portrayed as having their eyes rolled so far up into their foreheads that only the whites are visible. A connection between trance and this eye position was theorized.

Developed as part of a standard scale (the Hypnotic Induction Profile, Spiegel), the eye roll procedure is not only a means of measuring hypnosis but also a useful means of entering trance. The brisk approach in this method is particularly noticeable.

I'd like you to roll your eyes up into your forehead. That's it; keeping your head still, look straight up into your forehead.

The hypnotist may wiggle a forefinger at the very limits of the subject's upward peripheral vision to help attract the eyes up as far as they will go.

*Now, keeping your eyes up, I want you to slowly lower
the lids. Slowly close your eyes while the eyeballs remain
rolled up. Now, take a deep breath and hold it, hold it
. . . now let out the breath and relax your eyes, keeping
them closed until I tell you to open them. As your eyes relax, let that feeling of relaxation spread out over your
whole body.*

This induction often proceeds through a floating
sensation to an arm levitation. Reflecting the briskness
of this approach is the fact that if a subject's arm does
not move within a few seconds of the suggestion, the
hypnotist says, matter-of-factly, "Let's give it a little
help," and lightly gives a gentle tug to the subject's wrist.
The tug usually gets the levitation moving, although it
occasionally reveals the resistance of an arm that feels as
if it were nailed to the chair.

Rainbow

Some people are vividly aware of color and can feel it
almost as a mood. Using the spectrum in an induction is
a natural choice for such subjects.

*Feel yourself bathed in red, surrounded by red, then
moving through to orange and yellow . . . [through all
the colors of a rainbow]. Realize you are adrift in a
rainbow. By "violet" you will be fully relaxed and
hypnotized.*

33

Stairway

The image of descent found in this induction is useful because of the very common, preconceived notion that hypnosis is somehow "down." The direction probably comes from its long-time association with sleep ("fall asleep," "deep sleep"). Hypnosis is not, in fact, the same as sleep, and it is not "down" any more than it is "up."

> *Close your eyes. Imagine yourself on a stairway, a long, perhaps winding stairway. As you go down the stairs, counting them as you go, if you wish, you go down into hypnosis, deeper and deeper.*

Automatic Elevator

An induction for lazier subjects, but not for elevator phobics!

> *Close your eyes. Imagine yourself in an old-time elevator with the wheel-mounted handle that controls ascent and descent. You are the operator. Grab the handle. Pushing forward makes the car drop, pulling back makes it ascend. Control the depth of hypnosis this way.*

Counting

Any number will do, and the hypnotist can instruct the subject to count down instead of up.

> *Count up to ten. You will go deeper into hypnosis with each number until you reach your destination.*

Alphabet

This method is like "Counting," substituting letters for numbers. It might be used for "abecedarians" instead of mathematicians.

Exercise Bike

Relaxation is a common but not mandatory element of an induction. Subjects have been quite nicely hypnotized when riding a stationary exercise bike.

> *Start pedaling your bike. Feel the rhythm. As you continue to pedal, you will become hypnotized.*

DEEPENING TECHNIQUE

Occasionally, hypnotists like to use "deepening techniques" to increase the depth of trance. This technique is, very simply, a hypnotic induction done *after* hypnosis has been induced. The most common method is to suggest to the hypnotized subject that he open his eyes, focus on a target, and feel his eyes quickly become heavy enough to close.

Although degrees of participation in trance do vary, there are individual limits to how deeply hypnotized a person can become regardless of what techniques are used. That is, although there may be some increase in depth of trance, most likely because of the belief that the deepening technique will work, the limit to a person's hypnotic potential remains fixed.

TRICKS AND GIMMICKS

There are hypnotists who use paraphernalia such as strobe lights, metronomes, and spinning disks painted with a whirl to create a "hypnotic" atmosphere. One might as well add a baquet, a tub of iron filings, as in Mesmer's day, to concentrate the magnetism. Such props do little more than add an air of charlatanism to those who use them.

In fact, if one wanted to use a whirling disk or a slow, rhythmic metronome as the focus of an induction, the *imagining* of the stimulus would be far superior to the real thing. That is, the spoken words, "Imagine hearing a metronome, hear it slowly, steadily, rhythmically ticking, ticking, ticking, and with each tick, the sound becomes more real, and you become more and more hypnotized," are far more useful to a subject than a real metronome, which tends to become a nuisance.

STANDARD SCALES

Standard scales are a means of measuring hypnotizability. They include an induction and a set number of suggestions. The number of suggestions a subject follows is his score. Generally, lower numbers reflect a lesser degree of responsiveness to hypnosis, whereas higher numbers show a greater degree. These scales are designed to make the rating of response *objective* and to provide the reliable, valid standards necessary for research. Unlike the foregoing series of inductions, which can be adapted and varied, the induction portion of a standard scale remains unalterable. These inductions are read verbatim or are given by tape recording.

A standard scale is sometimes administered as a first or second experience with hypnosis. One rationale for using a scale early on is that many people underestimate their degree of responsiveness to hypnosis. If a therapist can tell a subject, "Your performance was average [above average, low but adequate, etc.] in comparison with the population in general," the subject may feel encouraged about his chances of successful hypnotic treatment.

The variety of items on the standard scales can also provide a useful screening device for the therapist. The response or lack of response to suggested tasks demonstrate what the subject can and cannot do. This knowledge, in turn, can help guide the hypnotist in choosing which therapeutic strategies to try first. Additionally, having a firm knowledge of a patient's responsiveness to hypnosis, rather than relying on a subjective hunch, can let the therapist know how much or how little to depend on hypnosis as an adjunct to psychotherapy.

For some potential subjects, the distrust and anxiety of interpersonal situations is so great that they cannot seem to let themselves go enough to enter hypnosis. In such cases, the Harvard Group Scale of Hypnotic Susceptibility may ease the entrance into hypnosis. Because this scale is administered by tape recording, the subject need not fear interpersonal dynamics. He or she can be reassured by the fact that thousands of other people have survived this test.

INDUCTIONS IN ACTUAL PRACTICE

An unknown stranger who appears and tells another person to close his eyes and relax hasn't much hope of inducing hypnosis. The first step in any induction, therefore, is the establishment of rapport between hypnotist and subject. The hypnotist and person he or she is dealing with must get to know each other.

It is important to note that regardless of a person's potential for trance, other factors are involved in turning that potential into a real hypnotic experience. The basic human capacities for trust and mistrust of others, the expectation that one will be met with kindness, goodness, and helpfulness, on the one hand, or will be taken advantage of, abused, and debased, on the other, enter into an individual's decision to permit hypnosis to take place. Unless subjects feel safe and trust the hypnotist, they will not allow trance to follow. Subjects who feel comfortable are available to participate in an induction.

The beginning of an induction does not demand fanfare and formal announcement. Often, a dialogue about the subject's prior experiences with trance, if any, and his hopes, fears, and expectations evolves into a near-monologue by the hypnotist. As the hypnotist calms fears and assuages doubts, the subject focuses more and more attention on this reassuring voice, and an induction is, in fact, under way. Any questions a subject might have should be asked before the "formal induction" begins. Otherwise a nagging concern may be so distracting that it interferes with the ability to enter a trance.

A successful hypnotist usually has an air of confidence and competence. It is vital for the practitioner to know exactly what he or she wants to do, but the performance of such plans need not be rote, mechanical, or lifeless. Generally, a hypnotist develops a "patter" that not only makes it possible to transmit the key intellectual ideas clearly, but also allows communication at a level other than the simple meaning of the words. Just as the tone and smooth flow of sounds from a parent provide more comfort to a baby than the words "rockabye baby" in and of themselves offer, so the flow of patter develops a rhythm and cadence that can be mesmerizing. Like patter, praise, encouragement, and repetition are useful in an induction. These elements help subjects to accept the hypnotist's interpretation of reality and to focus on what is being suggested.

There are times when a subject will report some problem with the induction or hypnosis. A good hypnotist will take the time to ask about it and straighten things out. For example, a therapist suggested that a hypnotized patient's arm was light. The arm floated up nicely. The patient was told that it would stay light until the therapist touched his arm. After trance ended, the therapist touched his elbow, but his arm stayed aloft. When he complained about this persistent floating, he was asked why it was still light. The patient informed the therapist that it was supposed to stay that way until a touch on the elbow returned it to normal. The therapist, claimed the patient, hadn't touched his arm. Obviously, it would have been witless to argue whether or not the touch had occurred. Rather, the therapist simply reached over, touched the man's elbow, and said, "Now it will feel the usual way, no longer light."

A hypnotist must be prepared to take charge of events. For instance, during a training seminar, two train-ees were told to practice inductions, taking turns as sub-ject and hypnotist. When one of them was to be the subject, she felt self-conscious and began to giggle in embarrassment. Her partner, believing hypnosis was a serious, slightly frightening business, told her to stop giggling. Naturally, this order made her laugh even more uncontrollably. Her partner became slightly panicky at having begun this event and was caught between the wish to hypnotize and the urge to laugh. The instructor took over at this point and did the obvious. She said, "You are feeling comfortable and relaxed and aware of how humorous the situation of hypnosis is. That's right, laugh with the humor of it. Laugh until the laughter is emptied and then stop. Whether you wish to continue to laugh, to stop, or to start again does not matter. It only shows your awareness of the humor of the situa-tion." Of course, the trainee soon ceased to laugh.

Sometimes, on completion of a trance, the subject reports still feeling a little bit hypnotized. This feeling, which usually passes quickly, is quite understandable, for one does not ordinarily move with knife-edged clarity or sharpness from any state of consciousness to another.

During the time that a subject is becoming ac-quainted with hypnosis, the therapist often offers one or more simple motor suggestions. Most use the suggestion that a hand and forearm will become light. "Hold both arms straight out in front of you, and imagine the hands are pulled together by a magnet," is another common suggestion for early encounters. There are two main reasons for these routine suggestions. First of all, they give the hypnotist a rough estimate of how a subject is responding to hypnosis. This response reflects stable factors, such as overall degree of hypnotizability, as well as more variable traits – how the subject is responding today and why. For example, a negativistic subject might report that instead of becoming light, his or her hand has become so heavy that it could not even voluntarily be lifted.

The other rationale for using these checking suggestions has to do with letting the subject know how hypnosis feels. Often, people report something like, "I was sitting here feeling good and relaxed, but I figured that wasn't hypnosis and I wasn't a good subject. Then, all of a sudden, my hand really began to feel light and float up. I knew there really was no helium balloon attached to it, but it sure felt like there was one. Then I knew that maybe I really was hypnotized." The simple motor test often provides a powerful demonstration of what is occurring in a less dramatic way internally. It lets one "see" hypnosis.

When a hypnotist does an induction, he or she wittingly or unwittingly sets up the style and pace of events. If the hypnotist drones, "You will slowly enter hypnosis," the subject will take a long time, and trying to hurry things up will feel like trying to run underwater. A brisk, lively approach, contrary to the popular caricature, can work very nicely, is not boring for the hypnotist, and, most important, leaves more time to *use* hypnosis for treatment.

41

3
History

Hypnotizability, considered as a potentially adaptive, innate human capacity, may have developed over the course of evolution as a survival trait. A Cro-Magnon man, for instance, who was mauled by a bear and who was overwhelmed by the agony of his wounds, would have no chance of escaping the animal. If, however, the same Cro-Magnon could dissociate himself from the experience of pain, he would be in a better position to fight or run. Lacking Bufferin or Novocain, this injured man could use his ability to tolerate discomfort while healing. If able to survive, he could pass along his genes, including the potential for hypnotizability, to his offspring.

In a similar vein, the berserk Viking warriors habitually entered a trance, shouting "Odin, Odin, Odin" as preparation for battle. These fierce warriors did not bother to wear armor in combat and were remarkable in their ability to remain oblivious even to very serious wounds. They appeared invulnerable to their enemies. The berserks' capacity for dissociation from pain during battle may have helped lead to victory and thus to the preservation of the fittest fighters.

Intentional and accidental uses of hypnosis can be found in abundance throughout the past. Shamans and medicine men tried to make the most of this ability in their healing. Sibyl, the oracle at Delphi, as well as countless other seers, went into a trance to utter prophecies. Even phenomena such as Saint Vitus' dance have a strong element of suggestion in them.

Hypnosis thus has a history probably as long as the history of mankind. As a specific therapy, however, it dates to the eighteenth century.

MESMER (1734 – 1815)

Franz Mesmer was an Austrian physician who interested himself in the broad array of eighteenth-century scientific advances and discoveries, being particularly fascinated by the link between magnetism and electricity. Searching for more effective methods of treating the ill, Mesmer tried to incorporate physics into his medical practice.

He studied with the Jesuit priest Maximillian Hell, from whom he learned how to cure his patients by placing magnets on the afflicted parts of their bodies. When Mesmer began magnetic treatments in his own right, he developed a theory to support such procedures. He thought that there was an ethereal fluid, connecting man and the celestial bodies, whose flow was influenced by magnetic fields. Where there was disequilibrium in the flow of the fluid, there was an affliction in the body. His treatment therefore consisted of having patients drink an iron tonic called chalybeates, followed by his rubbing their bodies with magnets. The magnets were supposed to attract the iron in the tonic, and thus to draw the chalybeates to the malfunctioning part of the body,

44

thereby restoring the proper flow of fluid between the patient and the planets.

In an age when physicians did not even listen to a woman's heartbeat lest they touch her breast, it is not surprising that Mesmer's patients, many of whom were women with conversion hysteria, got better. Their improvement probably was brought about by Mesmer's suggestions that the treatment would work and by the sexual excitement of having the doctor rub their bodies. The method itself provided for a discharge of sexual tension and thus lessened the need for a symptom.

Although frequently successful, Mesmer remained oblivious to the dynamics of his technique and ignored the role of suggestion and imagination. His continued reliance on an absurd theory which somehow worked in practice led him into a number of disputes.

For instance, Mesmer once borrowed a magnet from Father Hell and produced a cure with it. Both men claimed credit for this success, Hell declaring the important element in the cure was the magnet, which was *his*, and Mesmer suddenly announcing that the genius really lay in its use. In fact, Mesmer decided, the magnet itself was unnecessary; it was merely a prop. (In spite of this new position, however, Mesmer continued throughout his career to use iron and magnets.)

Mesmer now claimed that the forces that controlled the ethereal fluid were an organic equivalent of magnets acting upon inorganic iron. That is, just as iron was influenced by a magnet, so could the fluid be influenced by a magnetic personality. This special quality of "animal magnetism" was roughly the same as charisma or the ability to dominate. Different people had different amounts of animal magnetism. Sick people had very little. Strong-willed people had more. Mesmer, it was clear, had a great deal, probably more than anyone else.

In 1778 this magnetic man cured a pianist of her long-standing hysterial blindness. Her father, a court functionary, feared his daughter would lose her pension as she gained her sight. Soon, as a consequence of her father's distress, she became blind once more. Amid the great furor over this "failure," Mesmer was repudiated by the University of Vienna and left Austria.

Settling in France, Mesmer was extremely successful for the six years before his forced retirement. He established in Paris a salon over which he presided with extreme theatricality. For treatment sessions, Mesmer dressed in a lilac-colored cloak and carried an iron staff. Flashing mirrors and soft music created the proper atmosphere. Dramatically centered in the middle of the clinical stage was the baquet, filled with iron filings and water. Protruding bars were clasped by patients. As their expectant tension built to a peak, Mesmer would touch each patient with his iron rod, provoking "remedial" hysterical seizures.

The medical community at large did not tend to accept, to put it mildly, this theatrical healing art and made free with accusations of quackery. At last, several royal commissions were appointed to investigate the mesmeric phenomena. The most important of these commissions was headed by the U.S. ambassador to Paris, Benjamin Franklin. Joining him were Antoine Lavoisier, who discovered oxygen, and Dr. Joseph Guillotin, who died on the invention named after him.

The investigators looked rather thoroughly at Mesmer and at the methods derived from his theory. Since "magnetized" trees were supposedly curative, along with bathtubs, magnets, and personality, the commission designed a double-blind experiment to test the trees' effects.

The experimenters chose two trees of rather similar appearance. One was "magnetized"; the other was left alone. Patients were selected and told they would be brought to a magnetized tree for a cure. However, only half of them were directed to the "magnetized" tree. The rest went to the unmagnetized one.

If magnetic fields were useful in restoring the proper balance and flow of ethereal fluid, in accordance with mesmeric theory, only patients who went to the charged tree should have been helped. Skeptics, on the other hand, would have expected that neither tree would be beneficial.

What happened in fact was that some patients in both groups were cured or improved. That is, each tree helped some people, and neither tree was better than the other at the business of therapeutics.

Based on such studies, the commission concluded that "magnetism without the imagination produces nothing" (Kroger and Fezler, 1976). What these men of science inadvertently disclosed, and what they failed to recognize as important, was that the use of the imagination could indeed be curative. The investigators were equally unconcerned with another significant implication of the tree study: that the imaginative event must have occurred not as the result of something done to the patient by the operator (hypnotist) but through something done by the patient to himself. That is, since trees don't hypnotize people, people must hypnotize themselves.

Mesmer left a legacy rich in confusion and misunderstanding. The association of "animal magnetism" and "dominance" continues even today with the fallacy that "strong-minded" people make the best hypnotists. In fact, good hypnotic subjects make the best hypnotists because they have experienced what they are trying to convey. Much of the tarnish on the reputation of hypnosis dates back to Mesmer. He surrounded and obscured the essence of a genuine healing art with a lot of absurd theory and foolish mummery. In the two centuries since his time, serious thinkers have continued to cycle through periods of acceptance and rejection of hypnosis, alternately impressed with its therapeutic potential or repelled by its air of theatrical quackery.

PUYSÉGUR (1751 – 1825)

A devout follower of Mesmer, the Marquis de Puységur was a military man with a social conscience. He used "magnetism" as a means of easing the pain endured by his wounded soldiers. Also concerned with the large number of sick peasants who lived on his estates, but unable to treat so many individually, the Marquis "magnetized" a tree to which all might go for healing.

Puységur's historical importance lies in his observation and labeling of subjects who today would be referred to as being "at the top of a hypnosis scale" or "extremely responsive to hypnotic suggestion."

The Marquis correctly noted that such individuals could enter a deep trance and maintain this state undisturbed while carrying out a variety of tasks. He also observed that the suggestion of amnesia was frequently successful. Puységur was, however, diverted by the notion that such highly responsive people resembled sleepwalkers when entranced.

By coining the term *somnambules* for this group, Puységur helped to establish the mistaken notion that hypnosis is equivalent to sleep. By the same token, the old folklore surrounding sleepwalkers (e.g., that they can walk on dangerous ledges without loss of balance if not awakened) became attributable to hypnotic subjects.

Elliotson (1791 – 1868)

John Elliotson was a London physician who went to an exhibition of magnetism a skeptic and returned a convert. Announcing that hypnosis made it possible to establish a special, spiritual contact between himself and patients, he declared mesmerism a supernatural means of making accurate diagnoses. That is, hypnosis was supposedly something like taking a psychic X ray.

Elliotson founded the Mesmeric Hospital in London, began demonstrating the use of trance to control pain, and published *The Zoist*, a journal that reported current advances in mesmeric practice. Perhaps the most important bit of progress was the use of mesmerism as anesthesia during surgery. Before ether was introduced in 1864, hundreds of major operations, including amputations, were successfully performed under hypnosis.

The eighteenth-century discovery that surgery can be undergone with trance alone remains important in its implications about the nature of pain and hypnosis. The mind, then as now, has the potential to alter dramatically the perception of pain. (See chapter 10.)

Despite the immense usefulness of hypnosis in limited areas, Elliotson's claim of supernatural elements, and his unfortunate tendency toward self-aggrandizement, made him and his practices rather unpalatable in medical circles.

BRAID (1795 – 1860)

James Braid, a Scottish surgeon, noted that most trances occurred when the patient was relaxed, with eyes closed, and in a state superficially resembling sleep. Thus, he labeled this state "hypnosis," from Hypnos, the Greek god of sleep. He was quick to point out, however, that hypnosis was essentially different from sleep because the hypnotized subject was, in fact, quite awake and alert. Despite such disclaimers, the term itself has contributed to the confusion between sleep and hypnosis.

Braid did not understand why or how suggestion worked. Unlike other pioneers in the field, however, Braid never presented speculation as fact. Discarding all supernatural and exotic aspects of mesmerism, and rejecting all theories of magnetism or ethereal fluid, he dealt with the *science of hypnosis* in practical terms.

He observed that a high degree of concentration and narrowly focused attention was intrinsic to the hypnotized subject. Furthermore, he noted that the essential factor in trance must lie with the subject, not the hypnotist.

The first student of hypnosis to make it remotely reputable, Braid was also the prototype for the modern, respectable hypnotic investigator. That is, he opposed the cult of personality that often grows up around a charismatic hypnotist and focused on the subject's response, trying to integrate hypnosis with the large body of acceptable scientific knowledge.

CHARCOT (1825 – 1893)

A most important figure in dynamic psychotherapy, neurology, and hypnosis, Jean Martin Charcot demonstrated a capacity for careful clinical observation and documentation of his patients' illnesses. He identified and labeled multiple sclerosis and throughout his career studied a number of other neurological conditions. Among these disorders, Charcot was particularly interested in conversion hysteria.

Although conversion hysteria is now understood as a psychological conflict that shows itself in physical disability, Charcot believed it was a degenerative, hereditary, neurological disorder. He believed wholeheartedly in Mesmer's magnetism and ethereal-fluid theory of hypnosis. Theorizing that there was a relation between hysteria and hypnotizability, Charcot mistakenly explained that hypnotizability was an element of hysteria. Only hysterics, he claimed, could be hypnotized. Only they had the proper neurological defect which was the basis of the problem in the flow of ethereal fluid. This incorrect concept continues today as the myth that one can only be hypnotized if one has the diagnosis of hysteria.

One possible reason for the association is the fact that there are personality attributes in hysterics that may tend to make them, as a group, more able and willing to *use* whatever capacity for hypnotizability is available. People diagnosed as obsessives, on the other hand, may tend to keep a more rigid check on their hypnotic potential and thus be less willing or able to use it. However, primary suggestibility is a stable trait. It does not vary according to different types of diagnoses, any more than does intelligence, for instance.

Charcot's clinical observations were fortunately much more solid than his theories. Conducting a series of demonstrations at the Salpêtrière Hospital in Paris, he repeatedly hypnotized a great number of hysterics. From these demonstrations emerged the important fact that a variety of new hysterical symptoms could be produced and cured with hypnotic suggestion.

Charcot represents a significant transition between Mesmer and modern therapeutic hypnosis. Just as Braid brought trance from magnetism to hypnosis and introduced the subject as a science, Charcot brought the field of hypnosis into the realm of respectable medicine – specifically that branch of neurology that evolved into psychiatry.

JANET (1859 – 1947)

One of Charcot's most famous pupils, Pierre Janet adhered to his mentor's belief that hypnotizability was the key to hysteria and that a hereditary brain disorder was involved in this neurosis. Janet strongly rejected Mesmer's theory of magnetism, however, leaving Charcot the last serious scientist to accept that belief.

Janet proposed a new theory. He thought that in a hypnotic induction there was "a retraction of the field of personal consciousness and a tendency to the dissociation and emancipation of the systems of ideas and functions that constitute personality" (Janet, 1907). That is, a progressive dissociation occurred. Consciousness was suppressed and allowed for the emergence of the unconscious. This explanation continues to hold a major place in modern hypnotic theory and evolved into the idea that neurotic symptoms have an unconscious meaning.

BERNHEIM (1837 – 1919) AND LIÉBEAULT (1823 – 1904)

Named after their headquarters in France, the Nancy group of physicians was led by Ambroise-August Liébeault and Hippolyte-Marie Bernheim. Despite frequent disagreements, this pair remained in accord regarding two elements of hypnotic theory. They believed that hypnotizability was not limited to hysterics but could be demonstrated equally well on subjects with no such disorder. Their position that hypnotizability was a capacity possessed even by "normal" people led to a bitter feud with the Salpêtrière group, which refused to modify its original stance.

The Nancy group believed that the basis of hypnosis was the enhancement of suggestibility, the aptitude for turning thought into action. They began using this capacity not only to create new symptoms in hysterics, as did Charcot and Janet, but also to cure the original symptoms.

FREUD (1856 – 1939)

At a time when hypnosis was the leading edge of the psychoanalytic movement, Sigmund Freud emerged as the major influence on therapeutic technique. Having been taught by both masters in the field, Charcot and Bernheim, Freud returned to his native Austria to work with Josef Breuer. There they wrote *Studies in Hysteria*. These case histories demonstrated that at the root of hysterical symptoms were repressed memories that could be unlocked with hypnosis.

Freud, however, was not particularly comfortable as a hypnotist. The man who invented the analytic couch, which let him sit unseen, did not enjoy the intimate, knee-to-knee, physical style of hypnotic induction then in vogue. In fact, for some time he employed a technician to hypnotize patients, involving himself only after the patient was entranced. Freud was therefore pleased to discover that the technique of free association allowed access to repressed memories as well as, and often better than, hypnosis.

As Freud developed his theories and practices, his

enthusiasm for hypnosis waned until, finally, he repudiated it with a vengeance. He described hynotherapy as "mechanical drudgery – hodman's work – not scientific work." With hypnosis, he stated, the therapy might be more rapid, but the "results were capricious and not permanent." Hypnosis blocked the necessary understanding of dynamics. It did nothing to remove "resistance" (the force in the unconscious that tries to defeat attempts to cure). He warned that symptoms cured with hypnosis would return or would reappear in another form (symptom substitution) (Freud, 1924).

THE ECLIPSE AND REEMERGENCE OF THERAPEUTIC HYPNOSIS

The fact that trance was disgraced and discarded in favor of analytic technique was a tremendous setback for therapeutic hypnosis. It is unfortunate that hypnosis should have been rejected with as much fervor as analysis was embraced. Neither is the one and only perfect treatment for everything. Each is a treatment of choice for something different, and to say that one is better than the other is a bit like saying a comb is no good because you can't brush your teeth with it.

Freud was not alone in first using, then condemning, hypnosis. In nineteenth-century America, a young woman named Mary Baker sought help from a typical magnetizer named Quimby. She found so much relief that she began to work with him. Eventually, however, they quarreled, and she ended up describing magnetism as "the voluntary or involuntary action of error in all its forms." Instead, she declared, any good results found in using hypnosis were really the work of God. After marrying Mr. Eddy, she founded the Church of Christ, Scientist, on the revised principles learned from Quimby.

Such reversals have marked the history of hypnosis for the last two centuries. Its popularity has waxed and waned in respectable professional circles and among the more sensationalistic "true believers." There continue to be those who encourage the view of hypnosis as a mystical event. First are the charlatans, who have no professional status, but are esteemed solely as hypnotists. Heirs to Mesmer's mumbo-jumbo, these hypnotists act as the "initiated" who reveal bits of the "mystery" to the masses. Among professionals, too, there are, regrettably, those who become overly enamored of trance's effectiveness. They sometimes get so caught up in their successes that they lose sight of common sense and attribute each and every positive gain to hypnosis per se. Like Mesmer, Puységur, and Elliotson, they have lost scientific skepticism. Because their claims about hyponsis's potential are overinflated and because often they mix fantasy with more solid reasoning, hypnosis as presented by these practitioners is wide open to attack. Unfortunately, however, this justified criticism tends to be leveled at *all* of hypnosis, so that its positive effects are either ignored or denied.

Several times during its history, when hypnosis began to gain a foothold in medical practice, something would happen to undercut it. For instance, hypnosis began to rise in popularity when it was found to be a means of anesthesia. However, trance was soon discarded in favor of ether. Hypnosis simply did not work as well as this chemical. Ether works reliably on nearly 100 percent of the population; hypnosis on only a fraction of it. Furthermore, the late 1800s were a time when the field of medicine was growing along technological and specialized lines. As more was learned about diseases, doctors were more able to do something for sick patients – with vaccinations, new medicines, disinfectants, anesthesia. Hypnosis, unlike these much more tangible treatments, was quite dependent on the interaction between doctor and patient. More of the task of curing was left in the hands of the ailing person, rather than being in the doctor's control.

At one time, hypnosis enjoyed some deserved popularity in the treatment of psychological as well as physical symptoms. Freud led the field away from hypnosis to the point that it became considered a disreputable thing to do. When respectable people ignore or abandon a practice that in fact offers something positive, less respectable people tend to take it over. The fact that hypnosis was not regulated by law allowed quacks, charlatans, and entertainers access to the field. Thus, hypnosis became even more disreputable, discouraging interested professionals from associating themselves with it.

In recent times, the growing interest in hypnosis has paralleled a trend toward recognizing that technology by itself is not adequate to maintain health. Authoritarian doctors are no longer in vogue. People are increasingly encouraged to take charge of their health by adopting good habits of diet, exercise, and the like. Some modern physicians introduce themselves to patients as "the junior partner" in the enterprise of caring for the body. This trend is most clearly seen in the area of childbirth. Lamaze, midwifery, home birthing, and homelike birthing centers reflect a public and professional interest in the conjoint responsibility of doctor and patient. Hypnosis fits right into this popular philosophy. As a result, more and more respectable practitioners are using it. Being a hypnotist no longer means being a fringe cultist.

Contemporary professional societies (Society for Clinical and Experimental Hypnosis, International Society for Hypnosis, American Society of Clinical Hypnosis) require minimum credentials of training and education. They see hypnosis as an adjunct to the skills a practitioner already has. Hypnosis should be used only by physicians, psychologists, dentists, and clinical social workers who (1) are already proficient in their speciality, (2) have been subsequently trained in hypnosis, and (3) use hypnosis in the context of their profession.

The less acceptable, so called "ethical" hypnosis societies are typically made up of untrained individuals, many of whom have bought diplomas as "master hypnotists" for a substantial fee. Although competent individuals sometimes accidentally find their way into such groups, it is the exception, not the rule.

The popular perception of hypnosis is gradually evolving from myth and misunderstanding to a more realistic appreciation of its potential and limitations. If inflated claims can be replaced by sober assessment, and if the practice of hypnosis can be regulated to exclude vaudevillians, it may continue to find a significant place in the healing arts.

4
Twentieth-century Research

Following in the scientific tradition laid down by Braid, Janet, and the Nancy group, modern investigators have continued to explore hypnosis through a wide variety of studies and experiments. In the early part of this century, most of these studies related to a set of three fundamental ideas: (1) there really was an event known as hypnosis, (2) this event was some sort of psychological occurrence, not a physical event connected with magnetism, and (3) hypnosis was involved with imagination and "suggestion," although no one was quite clear what that term meant.

In much of the work done before 1940, scientists hazily described their observations or tried out various kinds of suggestions and then studied how they correlated with response to hypnosis. Such correlations were rough at best, since no reliable measure of response to hypnosis existed. Attempts to measure hypnotizability were rather like attempts to measure intelligence before Binet. People had a general idea that some people were smarter than others, but no quantitative scale existed.

One early attempt involving measurement of response to suggestions was the Postural Sway Test. (This test may be understood as a larger-scale version of the

Head Falling Forward suggestion in chapter 1.) A person would be told to stand erect, with eyes closed, feet together, and arms at sides. He would then be shown that he was in no danger of falling and being hurt, because the experimenters would catch him. He would be told repeatedly to imagine himself rocking back and forth or falling backward or forward.

Rather than relying on subjective judgments ("I'd say his sway was a *pretty far* on the scale from *still* to *very much sway*"), a measuring device was used. A piece of string was attached to the subject's shoulder with a pin. The string ran through a pulley to a piece of chalk on a chalkboard. (A variant method was to put a piece of chalk directly on the shoulder while the subject stood right next to the chalkboard.) As the person swayed, the string was pulled and released, making the chalk draw a line. The line could then be measured with a ruler and the results recorded.

What most excited the experimenters was the fact that as a large number of tests were recorded, the scores (the lengths of the chalk lines drawn) distributed themselves along a "normal curve." That is, the greatest number of scores clustered around the average score, and the further one moved from the average, the fewer scores there would be. Because many, many aspects of human makeup naturally distribute themselves in such a pattern, the researchers initially thought they had found a good test for hypnotic response.

As these tests proceeded, however, various flaws were discovered. For instance, women consistently tended to have lower scores than men. In fact, men and

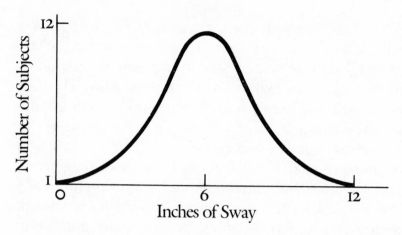

women each produced sets of scores that fit normal curves, with the average score for men higher than the average score for women.

It became clear, finally, that the length of the chalk line corresponded not only to the arc of sway but also to the length (height) of the person doing the swaying. Thus, the difference in male and female scores did not indicate that men had a greater capacity for hypnotizability than women but simply reflected the tendency of men to be taller than women.

Flaws in such test designs and interpretations were corrected, the susceptibility scales of the 1930s were modified, and eventually the concept of measuring observable hypnotic behavior evolved into today's standardized scales of hypnotizability: the Stanford Hypnotic Susceptibility Scales (1959), the Harvard Group Scale (1962), and other, more recent scales.

These scales all had a number of features that attracted researchers. They involved nonsubjective ratings. Time could be measured by a stopwatch, distance by a ruler. Different examiners could compare ratings in a reliable way, with clear criteria for judgment. The behavior that was rated – response to hypnotic suggestions – made sense as an indication of hypnotizability. The tests objectified and formalized what hypnotists routinely did to assess response.

These standard scales were designed to include a hypnotic induction followed by a variety of suggestions that a subject either performed or failed to perform. For instance, a subject was instructed to hold his hands out in front of his body, palms facing inward and twelve inches apart. It was then suggested that his hands would feel as though a force were pulling them together. If his hands moved to within six inches of each other in ten seconds, the item was scored as passed. If over six inches separated his hands at the ten-second mark, it was scored as failed. (See *Sample Scale of Hypnotizability* for typical suggestions and scoring criteria.)

The items on scales of hypnotizability were designed to reflect varying degrees of difficulty. That is, some items were supposed to be passed by most people, other items passed by only a few.

The number of suggested actions or experiences on these scales varied from four to seventeen, twelve being the most common, and a subject's score was the total number of these test items passed. This raw score would then be put into a gross ranking of low, average, or high.

These scales produce quite stable results, whether given individually or in groups, scored by an observer or by one's own self, taken twenty years ago or today. People who score at a certain level tend to maintain that level when retested hours or years later. Such constancy of scores indicates that hypnotizability, like intelligence, is a stable personality trait.

Just as in the testing of intelligence, both anxiety and unfamiliarity with the testing procedure are now known to result in lower scores. Therefore, any modern researcher who is concerned about the accuracy of a score will establish a baseline by measuring a subject's response on two or even three scales. It should be noted that the score which is then used as an estimate of the subject's level of response is *not* his average score, but rather the score on the *last* test. The assumption underlying this method is that a person becomes increasingly comfortable with and adept at entering a hypnotic state as he is increasingly exposed to it.

Twenty years before the introduction of these standardized scales, researchers were exploring the nature of "suggestibility" by giving huge numbers of established tests of perception, motivation, and personality, while at the same time giving the subjects varieties of suggestions, and then seeing what correlated with what. Out of this empirical mishmash emerged the division of "suggestibility" into three types: primary (the only kind associated with hypnotizability), secondary, and tertiary.

The clearest definition of secondary suggestibility was found in a study involving the Progressive Weights Test. A dozen blocks were put out in a specified manner. The first six blocks were ordered in sequence so that each one was heavier (or lighter) than the one before it. Each subject was then asked to pick up the first and second blocks, the second and third, and so on, and compare

SAMPLE SCALE OF HYPNOTIZABILITY

Passive Motor Items

1. POSTURAL SWAY: "Close your eyes, put your feet together, imagine swaying." *Score + if subject allows himself to lose his balance.*

2. HEAD FALLING FORWARD: "Think about how it would feel to let your head fall forward." *Score + if chin goes to chest.*

3. EYE CLOSURE: "Stare at a spot; your eyes feel heavy and close by themselves." *Score + if eyes closed before specified time.*

4. ARM LOWERING: "Hold out your arm. Imagine it feels very heavy, as though you were holding a lead weight. Feel it pulled down." *Score + if arm moves down six inches in 10 seconds.*

5. ARM LEVITATION: "Imagine that your arm is very light, as if attached to a helium balloon." *Score + if arm goes up six inches in ten seconds.*

6. MOVING HANDS TOGETHER: "Hold hands straight out in front of you, palms inward. Imagine magnets pulling your hands toward each other." *Score + for moving six inches in ten seconds.*

7. POST HYPNOTIC SUGGESTION: "After trance is over, touch your ankle when you hear a tap. You will do this without remembering these instructions." *Score + if done.*

Challenge Suggestion Items

1. ARM IMMOBILIZATION: "Your arm, resting on the arm rest of chair, is heavy and limp, too heavy to lift. Just try to lift it." *Score + if arm is not raised in ten seconds.*

2. FINGER LOCK: "Hold hands out in front of you, tightly interlocking your fingers so that they cannot be separated. Now try to separate them." *Score + if fingers are still intertwined after ten seconds.*

3. ARM RIGIDITY: "Extend your arm and lock it into a straight position. Imagine it is an iron bar. Try to bend it." *Score + if arm is unbent after ten seconds.*

4. COMMUNICATION INHIBITION: "You are so relaxed that you cannot shake your head no. Now just try to shake your head no." *Score + if subject doesn't shake head before ten seconds.*

5. EYE CATALEPSY: "Your eyes are so tightly shut they cannot be opened. Just try to open them." *Score + if eyes stay closed for ten seconds.*

Imagery Items

1. DREAM: "Have a real dream." *Score + if dreamlike experience happened, not just flashing images or consciously controlled scenes.*

2. AGE REGRESSION: "Remember, then go back into the past to a pleasant day in childhood at school." *Score + if past is recalled with good visual images and, if not feeling as though in the past, the subject is at least feeling as though the experience was more vivid than simple memory.* Variant scoring: *Have subject write name at earlier ages. See if handwriting regresses, e.g., from cursive to printing, from married to maiden name.*

3. HALLUCINATED TASTE: "Imagine you taste salt." *Score + if taste is reported.*

4. SMELL INSENSITIVITY: "Imagine you cannot smell." *Score + if there is no sign of response to ammonia waved under nose.*

5. NEGATIVE VISUAL HALLUCINATION:
(*Three* blocks are placed on a table.) "When you open your eyes, you will see *two* blocks. Open your eyes and see how many blocks there are." *Score + if only two blocks are reported.*

6. AUDITORY HALLUCINATION: "Another [imagined] experimenter will be asking you questions about your age, height, and hair color when I stop talking." *Score + if subject begins giving answers when all is silent.*

7. FLY HALLUCINATION: "Imagine a fly is buzzing around you very annoyingly." *Score + if subject moves to shoo it away.*

Memory Item

POSTHYPNOTIC AMNESIA: "Upon the end of trance, it will be too hard for you to recall the items on this test until you are told to remember." *Score + if less than a third of the items are recalled before the subject is told to remember.*

Score is total number of items scored +.

their relative weights. The subjects were able to note the pattern and, by the sixth block, were sure of what would come next. Now, in fact, the anticipated pattern did not continue. Blocks seven through twelve were of identical weight.

Some subjects, however, knowing that the tendency was to increase (or decrease) weight progressively, reported that they observed a relative increase (or decrease) in the remaining cubes.

These subjects had responded to the suggestion intrinsicially given by the pattern of the first six blocks. They had perceived in the final six blocks something that was not really there and had thus experienced an alteration in perception. What they had not done, however, was make a conscious, willing decision to cooperate in such a distortion. If the experimenter had suggested, "Imagine that blocks seven through twelve will grow increasingly heavy [or light]," and if a willing subject had then experienced the blocks to weigh accordingly more or less, the subject would have been using his capacity for primary suggestibility.

Instead, these subjects were demonstrating a different trait. The distortion of perception based on expectation – that is, the tendency first to think that something will be a certain way and consequently to perceive it so – was called secondary suggestibility.

A further differentiation among the three types of suggestibility was illustrated by another experiment. In this study, seven participants were brought into a room and shown sets of lines. In each set of four lines, there was one standard line, X, and three comparison lines, A,

B, and C. The subjects were asked to match line X with the one comparison line that was its identical twin – B, in this example.

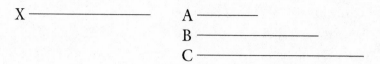

Now, of the seven individuals involved in this experiment, only one was a real subject and the actual focus of the study. All of the other participants were in fact stooges working with the investigators. These six "subjects" would, as arranged, match blatantly dissimilar lines – for instance, A with X.

The point of the experiment was to find out if the actual subject would go along with the crowd and accept the group verdict rather than follow the evidence of his own senses. Some did and some did not. Among those who yielded were subjects who knew, to varying degrees, that A was not the same as X. Some of these individuals took the attitude that since this was only an experiment, it didn't matter if A was the wrong answer. It was easier to agree with the group than stand up against the crowd. Other subjects, however, began seriously to doubt their own perceptions as the pressure to conform mounted. Initially stating that B was identical to X, they changed their minds, citing such possibilities as optical illusion, angle of view, or previously undetected eye trouble to rationalize their original answers.

The tendency to follow the crowd in this fashion, to switch, for instance, from Canada Dry club soda to Perrier, to respond to social pressure or authority by doubting, then disowning, one's verdicts and judgments in order to accept the group consensus, was called tertiary suggestibility. The story of "The Emperor's New Clothes" would be a classic example.

Researchers in the 1940s discovered that the presence or absence of either tertiary or secondary suggestibility was in no way indicative of nor related to the presence or absence of primary suggestibility. According to these researchers, primary suggestibility, although easily confused with other, unrelated personality factors, was *not* the same as persuadability, gullibility, a response to social pressure or cues, a tendency to follow the crowd, or a yielding to the lure of advertising. They defined primary suggestibility as the capacity to *choose* to distort perception or experience in line with suggestions that such changes would occur. It was seen to be not only the sole kind of suggestibility that had anything to do with hypnosis, but also the basic element underlying the phenomenon of hypnosis.

In the 1960s, researchers reexamined the information gathered in these 1940s studies, ran old data through computers, and came up with a refinement of the concept of primary suggestibility. Several slightly different but related facets of primary suggestibility were defined. Each was an element of hypnotizability, the investigators stated. All might be found together in various degrees, and they reflected some of the different ways people responded to hypnosis.

The first of these facets was labeled *passive motor suggestibility* and was defined as the occurrence of a physical motion or sensation in response to the suggestion of motion or sensation. An arm feeling light enough to float up in the air is an example of such an occurrence.

The term *challenge suggestibility* applied to the coupling of a passive motor suggestion with a contradictory order. That is, a person was first told to imagine an action or sensation, then was instructed to try to overcome that imagined action or sensation. It was hoped that the person would perceive the contradictory order as the one to be disobeyed. For instance, the suggestion "Feel that your arm is heavy, so heavy it would be impossible to pick it up" could be followed by "Just try to pick it up, just try." The real order is to try to pick up the arm and *fail to do so*.

The capacity to distort vividly perceptual experience rather than motor activity was called *imagery suggestibility*. Hallucinations, dreamlike states, and disorientation fall under this heading.

Finally, alteration of memory, either loss of memory (amnesia) or increased capacity for memory (hypermnesia), was included as an element in the constellation known as *primary suggestibility*.

The capacity for primary suggestibility was known to be enhanced by hypnosis, and as early as 1917 investigations were being made as to what might facilitate, hasten, or otherwise affect the speed and depth of induction and trance. Often used in these studies were the "hypnotics" (sleep-inducing drugs). Because the research methods used early in this century were so sloppy, more modern scientists could not rely on the reports of generally positive results. Accordingly, more controlled work was done, using alcohol, marijuana, LSD-25, and mescaline. Participants in these studies were given tests of hypnotizability (1) after a hypnotic induction, (2) while drugged but not hypnotized, and (3) while drugged as well as hypnotized. Their scores tended to be the same in all three states. That is, either hypnosis or certain drugs will increase hypnotizability to the same extent, but the effects are not additive. The capacity for enhanced suggestibility can be activated by a number of agents, but because suggestibility is one single trait, once activated, it is useless to add extra activators.

How much of this trait was present in what kind of personality formed the basis of another track of research. It was assumed for years, à la Charcot, that hysterics were more hypnotizable than people with other kinds of personalities. It was also taken for granted that the higher one's intelligence and intellectual level of functioning were, the less responsive one would be to suggestion. To allow oneself to be hypnotized seemed akin to admitting, "I'm so dumb I'll believe anything you suggest."

In the 1960s, roughly 500 people were tested in an effort to determine which qualities were associated with various degrees of hypnotizability. Tests measured demographic data, personality traits, psychiatric diagnosis, intelligence, and personal history as well as hypnotizability.

Not surprisingly, hypnotic response correlated with traits that are now known as elements of hypnosis. Having an imaginary playmate as a child and the capacity to become completely absorbed by music, reading, or the theater were associated with hypnotizability. Also to be expected was the finding that some basic trust is a *sine qua non* of trance. One cannot sit back and experience hypnotic suggestions while constantly on the lookout for abuse.

Nothing else was found that predicted high or low hypnotic responsiveness. The capacity for hypnotizability is a trait that exists regardless of sex, intelligence, psychiatric diagnosis, and character or cognitive style.

Personality has, then, basically no influence on hypnotizability. However, the influence of hypnosis on personality has been an issue for years. In 1939, an interesting study was done at an Ivy League university. Psychology undergraduates were recruited to participate in this experiment.

Subjects were first shown a container of poisonous snakes. Next, the experimenter dissolved a penny in a beaker of liquid, demonstrating that the beaker held an extremely corrosive acid. The students were then hypnotized.

While in a trance, each subject was given two commands: (1) to handle a dangerous snake and (2) to throw the beaker of acid into the face of the experimenter's assistant.

It was confidently anticipated that these undergraduates would refuse to perform either task. To the contrary, however, the subjects were happily willing both to jam their hands into a potentially lethal container and to toss acid into the assistant's face.

No one was physically injured because the container was cleverly designed to prevent any possible contact between hands and fangs, and a harmless fluid had been substituted for the acid before it could be thrown. The experimenters, however, were quite dismayed. They concluded from the results of this study that they had exposed the potentially dangerous nature of hypnosis. It appeared as if the essential independence and goodness of the human spirit were threatened by the ability of one man to control or alter another.

Uncomfortable with the philosophical implications of continuing to support the practice of hypnosis, experimenters replicated this study in 1952. The results were no different the second time around.

In the 1960s, investigators in the field carried out a third study. It followed the design of the first in every detail but one: at no point were the subjects hypnotized. However, when they were given the commands to handle a snake and to throw acid, the students willingly obeyed.

Since no trance was involved in this experiment, hypnosis clearly could not be used to explain the subjects' uncharacteristically destructive behavior. The puzzled experimenters asked the participants why they had been willing to carry out such outrageous orders. They replied that because they were enrolled at a respectable university and were participating in research sponsored by the school's psychology department, they intuitively assumed that they would not be allowed to harm themselves or another. It was the nature of the experimental situation itself, not the hypnosis, which led to extraordinary compliance.

The ethical issues these experiments raised were similar to those involved in the well-known Milgram studies. In the latter case, subjects were ordered to deliver painful electric shocks to a person in the next room. Many subjects did so, not knowing that there were no real shocks administered or that the audible cries of pain and pleas for mercy were simulated.

Interest in these questions of free will and obedience was heightened by the horror of the Holocaust. People wanted to know if Americans could ever act like Nazi camp guards. It was found that, just as in the study of hypnosis and destructive behavior, the undesirable actions were the result of the experimental situation. "If a person really wanted someone to help him with an antisocial act, he should try to convince [that person] that he is participating in an experiment," observed one expert, half in jest (Coe et al., 1972). It is reassuring to know that current committees on the use of human subjects are designed to protect people from dangerous or upsetting experiments, and they would probably not permit such studies to be done now.

Hypnosis does not alter the personality, and personality does not alter hypnotic potential, but expectations on the part of the hypnotist and the subject do influence hypnotic behavior. A 1950s study demonstrated this point.

A professor lectured on hypnosis to two sections, A and B, of the same undergraduate psychology course. He used identical lectures for each section. Both sections were to include a demonstration induction with one of two preselected subjects. These two subjects had both been hypnotized prior to their scheduled class appearances. However, one of these subjects had been told, during his previous out-of-classroom induction, that whenever he was hypnotized, his right arm would become light and float up in the air. The other demonstration subject was told nothing about how his arm would behave following induction.

With no prompting, the first subject's arm did float up while the professor demonstrated hypnosis to section A. In section B, the subject's arm stayed still.

Following these demonstrations, students from both sections of the class were invited to participate in an experiment involving hypnosis. Those who attended section A had their arms float up while entranced although such a motion had never been verbally suggested to them. For the most part, the right arm was afloat. A few left-handed students, however, reasoned that it was the dominant arm that grew light, so their left arms went up. Members of section B showed no tendency for either arm to float.

It was suspected that motivation and compliance, like expectation, influence hypnotic behavior. In fact, some theoreticians maintained, and still do maintain, that there was no such event as hypnosis at all, simply behavior or experience based on other influential elements. A series of studies in the 1960s debated the point.

In one such series, the ability to tolerate pain was used to demonstrate the effects of various influences on hypnotic behavior. First, tolerance of pain was measured in the following manner: a blood pressure cuff was put on a subject and inflated until circulation to the forearm was cut off. At that point, the subject took a hand pump in the affected hand and began pumping water from one tank to another. This exercise caused pain, as there was no blood flow to replenish oxygen and sugar (for energy) and to carry off lactic acid and other breakdown products. The more exercise, the more water pumped, the greater the pain. When a subject could no longer bear it, he stopped pumping and unfastened the blood pressure cuff. The restored circulation quickly cured the pain, and the amount of water pumped could be used as a measure of pain endured.

Next the subjects were hypnotized. Having been given the hypnotic suggestion of analgesia to increase pain tolerance, they repeated the pumping exercise. Not surprisingly, it was found that their capacity to bear pain was greater with hypnosis than without it.

Those skeptical of the effects of hypnosis argued that the very use of hypnosis made the subjects expect increased pain tolerance. Additionally, critics declared, since the subjects felt that the experimenters wanted them to improve under hypnosis, they were motivated to tolerate more pain.

In an effort to test out this position, the study was replicated, with one difference: a pep talk was substituted for hypnosis. Sure enough, pain tolerance increased with the verbal boost. This result was used as proof that hypnosis was nothing but enhanced motivation.

Those maintaining the original view that *hypnosis* was what mattered designed yet another study. They took members of a football team, measured pain tolerance, and then split the players into two groups. Both groups were given a motivational push: "The cheerleader squad did better than you guys. Try it again, and this time don't be sissies." In addition to this motivational gibe, one of the two groups of players was given hypnotic suggestions of increased pain tolerance.

While both of these groups showed marked improvement over their original scores, the hypnosis group's increase was much greater than that of the other group.

This finding, however, did not settle matters. It was argued that the hypnosis group's improvement was attributable to a placebo effect. (That is, if people are given any treatment that is supposed to have a positive effect (pills, hypnosis, etc.), the treatment will have an effect on a predictable percentage of the population simply because it is believed to be effective.) Other researchers suggested that if hypnosis was not simply a placebo, perhaps hypnotizability was at the root of the placebo effect.

In the 1970s a fairly complicated, definitive study on pain relief quieted this debate. A large number of people were tested, each under a variety of different conditions. Motivation, hypnosis, placebo, and two or three of these variables in every possible combination were all compared, for subjects who were easily and deeply hypnotized as well as for those who were less responsive.

The experimenters found that, regardless of which other determinants were involved, people who were good hypnotic subjects could tolerate more pain when hypnotized than when they were not. Furthermore, good hypnotic subjects got more relief than did subjects with less hypnotic potential. Consistently, hypnosis helped to control pain, and the better hypnotic subjects got more pain control than less responsive people. Therefore, hypnosis was shown to be an agent with its own effective potential.

At roughly the same time as this finding emerged, researchers were also working to find a foolproof way of determining the presence or absence of hypnosis. Seemingly hypnotized people would say they were not hypnotized, or that they weren't sure one way or another, and it was possible to claim to be hypnotized while in fact not being hypnotized at all.

Early in this century, if a famous (or even a not so famous) doctor declared a person hypnotized, his clinical expertise was trusted over any contradictory indications. Later, tests were designed to see whether or not doctors could detect frauds. For example, five volunteers were found and told they were going to participate in a study to show that a doctor could distinguish a really hypnotized person from a fraud. Three of these volunteers would then be told to let themselves be hypnotized, and two were instructed to remain unhypnotized but to fake it. The problem with this study was that these latter two subjects expected to get caught faking. Accordingly, they hammed it up, giggled, and obviously shammed. The doctor could easily spot them, and thus his skill as an expert was "proved."

In the 1970s, an experiment was designed along these same lines, but with more solid research methods. The investigators took two groups of people: (1) those who scored 0 on a scale of hypnotizability and (2) those who scored at the top of the scale. Both of these groups were shown videotapes demonstrating good subjects experiencing hypnosis. Following the films, however, the two groups were separated and given different instructions. The good hypnotic subjects were told to allow themselves to be hypnotized by the experimenters' resident expert.

Teaching assistants worked with the group of unresponsive subjects. These helpers enlisted the subjects as allies in a plot to "fool the old man." The subjects were to *pretend* hypnosis when the expert attempted induction. It was expected that, since they had seen the videotapes, they would be able to mimic trance convincingly. In fact, when the expert did "hypnotize" them, he could not distinguish these fakers from the really responsive subjects.

Since expert observation had shown itself to be unreliable, researchers experimented with a variety of physical tests to differentiate hypnosis from nonhypnosis. Measures such as the EEG aroused early optimism since certain changes were found to occur regularly in hypnosis. It became clear, however, that such changes could also be produced by other means. In fact, there is no physical change found in hypnosis that cannot be found outside of hypnosis or that must always be exhibited during hypnosis.

Eventually it was decided to study large numbers of truly good subjects and subjects who were only good at faking it, then to see what differences, if any, emerged. Pools of very responsive and very unresponsive people were shown videotaped examples of good hypnotic subjects in a trance. They were then put into one of three groups: (1) poor subjects who were told to pretend to be hypnotized, but not to be so in fact, (2) good subjects who were told to allow themselves to be hypnotized, and (3) good subjects who were told not to allow themselves to be hypnotized, but to pretend to be.

In many ways the groups turned out to be indistinguishable. Some patterns of differences did show up, however. When something "went wrong," such as a "power failure," and the experiment's hypnotist left the room muttering about "seeing what happened," the fakers stayed in their "trance" for a long time awaiting the hypnotist's return. Truly hypnotized good subjects, on the other hand, stayed in trance for a bit, then common sense took over. They realized something was wrong, opened their eyes, ending the trance, and went out looking for the hypnotist, as if to say, "I may be hypnotized, but I'm not infinitely patient."

In another test situation, subjects were given, in trance, an arcane bit of knowledge, such as the population of Hong Kong or the effect of heating an amethyst. They were told they would have amnesia for this session of hypnosis. Later, unhypnotized, these subjects were asked the population or heating questions. Fakers vehemently denied any such knowledge. Good subjects answered readily. When asked how they knew such facts, they stated they didn't know how, made light of it, said, "Doesn't everyone know that?," or confabulated a source – "I was reading an article on Hong Kong in *National Geographic* last month. It must have mentioned the population."

At yet another point in the study, a chair was placed in the center of a room, and it was suggested that the subjects would not see it. When asked to open their eyes to look around the room, all subjects reported seeing nothing. They were then asked to cross the room. The fakers would walk straight into the chair with exclamations of, "What! I don't see anything," and keep banging into it. Good subjects, on the other hand, would calmly walk around the chair when crossing the room. When asked why they had steered clear of that spot, they denied avoiding it, just as they denied seeing the chair. They might not have seen it, but that didn't mean they had to walk into it.

Logic differs from the usual when one is hypnotized. For instance, a person, whom we shall call Dr. Jones, was seated on a subject's right. An empty chair was placed to the subject's left. It was suggested that the subject would see Dr. Jones in the chair to the left. All subjects did claim to see Dr. Jones on their left. However, when asked who then was that in the chair to the right, the fakers would say "No one," "A stranger," or "What chair?" Good subjects would reply "Dr. Jones." "But how," the hypnotist would ask, "can you see Dr. Jones in two places at once?" "I just do!" would be the answer. If asked whether the two Dr. Joneses differed in any way from one another, the good subjects might answer, "Well, I can see the chair through the Dr. Jones on the left. He's kind of transparent."

The ability to accept unquestioningly and without conflict, to see ideas that are mutually exclusive as concurrently true, is called *trance logic*. Highly responsive subjects grant to the hypnotist the responsibility to define physical sensation and logic. "If the hypnotist says Dr.

Jones is here, and I see him there," a good subject might think, "then there must be two of him." The presence or absence of trance logic became a good test for distinguishing between hypnotized subjects and simulators.

One interesting bit of information was gleaned from observations made of group 3, good hypnotic subjects who were told not to allow trance but to fake it. Following a completed hypnotic session, they were asked if they had slipped into hypnosis. All said no, although they had responded like truly hypnotized subjects. The investigators concluded that a good subject who goes through the motions of behaving *like* a hypnotized person is in fact hypnotized. It is probably something like pretending to read. If a literate person were to pretend to read printed pages, he would probably read them in fact. The only way to pretend convincingly is to *do* it.

Just how hypnosis is done, exactly *how* it happens, remains speculative. It has been proposed that hypnosis is an archaic transference (in the Freudian sense), a learned state, a version of sleep, a conditioned response, or a state in which the reticular formation (the part of the brain stem that screens stimuli) is involved. So far, however, none of these theories as to the actual mechanisms of the hypnotic process has been solidly substantiated.

What has been established during this century is a better understanding of the context and certain ingredients of hypnosis. It is a state of consciousness that occurs naturally. It is experienced in different ways in different degrees by different people. It is something one does to oneself. It involves concentration, attention, and imagination. It includes the abdication of the usual reality-orienting faculties and allows their transference to another part of the self. It is an enhancer of a stable personality trait, primary suggestibility.

Part II
Hypnosis and
Psychotherapy

"I can't believe that," said Alice. "Can't you?" the Queen said in a pitying tone. "Try again; draw a long breath and close your eyes."

Lewis Carroll
Through the Looking Glass

5
When Is Hypnosis Useful?

The rest of this book will discuss when hypnosis should be used, under what specific circumstances it can help, and which strategy is appropriate for each problem. The treatments described in the upcoming chapters, however, are not therapeutic blueprints. There are no set formulas for correct treatments, no verbatim instructions to be followed. Clinical practice and style vary from one practitioner to the next. The methods presented are, therefore, only a sample from a variety of possible approaches.

The cases described in the next set of chapters are not accurate portrayals of real people. Instead, the cases are composites of patients seen by the authors, seen by therapists supervised by the authors, or reported in the literature. All have been disguised so that the end result is a picture of a *type* of person and/or problem, not of a specific patient's therapy.

Both the individual in search of help and the therapist considering the use of hypnosis in practice should remember that hypnosis and the ability to induce trance are not in themselves curative. They are, instead, *adjuncts* to therapy. A dentist might use hypnosis as a means of reducing his patient's pain and anxiety. It is not his hypnotic skill, however, but his dental training that lets him fill a cavity. For a psychotherapist, hypnosis is simply one more technique in a variety of treatment strategies. Often, the use of hypnosis in therapy is simply a stylistic preference. It is not a substitute for therapeutic skill. Therefore, a person in search of treatment for a psychological or medical problem should beware of any practitioner who claims to offer a cure through hypnosis alone.

Each patient's expectations and preferences regarding hypnosis must always be considered. Sometimes it happens that a person does not wish to be hypnotized, whereas the hypnotist thinks hypnosis is the ideal treatment. In such cases certain effects associated with hypnosis, specifically those stemming from relaxation and imagination, can be brought about without the formal use of trance.

The application of clinical hypnosis within the context of ongoing, traditional psychotherapy can be complicated. Hypnosis used to treat a symptom that emerges during the course of therapy is, in some ways, analogous to medicine prescribed for symptomatic relief. Often it is helpful to clear up the symptom so that therapy can proceed.

For instance, a woman suffers from *agoraphobia* (fear of leaving her house). Her symptom has developed because she is unknowingly troubled by "unacceptable" instincts and impulses, and her conflict needs to be resolved so that the basis for the symptom disappears. Such resolution is the domain of long-term psychotherapy. Meanwhile, however, she is hardly able to leave her house to get to that therapy. Hypnosis would give her enough immediate symptomatic relief so that the needed long-term treatment could take place on a less desperate footing.

In cases like this one, where the first order of business is symptom relief, the early "cure" tends to make the later work quite productive since the therapist is viewed as helpful and effective. However, there is a radical difference between the actively controlling stance of the hypnotist, who tells his patient how to sit and breathe, what to think and how to feel, and the more passive, less directive style of the traditional psychotherapist, who sits back and says, "Tell me what is on your mind." It is important that the reasons for these changes in therapeutic stance be clearly spelled out. Otherwise, the patient may be distressed when a formerly talkative, active hypnotist suddenly becomes a quiet, nondirective therapist. The shift back and forth between these stances, along with the resulting intensification of emotion, can be difficult for both of the people involved. Therefore, no matter how skilled a hypnotist he or she may be, the therapist may decide it is best to refer the patient to a colleague for any hypnotic treatment.

There continues to be a debate about the use of hypnosis with people who are psychotic. Some clinicians consider it a prime treatment mode for psychosis. Other therapists hold that it is risky to treat someone who is paranoid or whose reality testing is in some other way deficient, by asking him to trust a hypnotist who intentionally further distorts reality. With psychotics it is possible to use a conservative modification of hypnotic treatment that focuses on the simple element of relaxation and avoids any reality-distorting suggestions. In any case, when thinking is severely disordered, the degree and kind of concentration necessary for hypnosis often are lacking, rendering the question moot.

During Freud's original infatuation with hypnosis, trance was used as an integral, ongoing part of long-term therapy. Once widespread, such hypnotherapy is now practiced less often, primarily because it does not remove a patient's resistance to treatment. Without a patient's conscious and unconscious compliance, any treatment is doomed to failure.

There are times when, nonetheless, hypnosis may be woven into the fabric of ongoing psychotherapy. Trance can be used to enhance psychoanalytic or psychotherapeutic technique. For example, some patients in psychoanalysis have much difficulty giving up enough control to free-associate. In trance, these people may find it more permissible or easier to allow a free flow of ideas. The analyst, in such cases, might suggest to the hypnotized patient that he or she talk about whatever comes to mind. If a memory is to be discussed, the analyst might suggest strengthening the recall by age regression. This strengthening would not necessarily provide more accurate information about the patient's past, but it would help make the recall more vivid and available. (It should be noted that just as a nonhypnotized analysand does not remember repressed material until enough work has been done to allow it to be remembered, so the hypnotized analysand is unlikely to recall material for which the proper groundwork has not been laid. Hypnosis does not accelerate this process.)

Similarly, hypnosis can be used for the dream work that is commonly a part of psychotherapy. A therapist might suggest to a hypnotized patient that the patient is about to have a dream. He or she might then suggest that it will feel like a real dream and will be related to the work of therapy. The patient is instructed, finally and most importantly, to remember the dream *so that it may be discussed*.

These hypnotic suggestions may be useful to any patient who has difficulty dreaming, producing fantasies, or allowing unconscious material to reach consciousness. However, the *curative* factor here is the therapeutic work that follows. When a patient produces a dream (or daydream, thought, etc.) in trance, it is not really different from other nighttime dreams (or daydreams, thoughts, etc.) that the patient describes to the therapist in the next regular session. The difference lies in the fact that hypnosis seems to enhance permission for producing such material. Thus it can be helpful for patients who are blocked or excessively guilty over their own thoughts and feelings.

Hypnosis is particularly well suited for treating problems whose geneses may have involved hypnotizability. Thus, fugue states, which can resemble trance, some kinds of fear or panic, which are experienced as distortions of reality, and some memory disorders would be theoretically amenable to hypnotic treatment. Additionally amenable would be destructive habits for which the cure requires new learning. Because what needs to be relearned can be practiced again and again by imagining, hypnosis would hypothetically be a choice treatment for habit control.

However, even if hypnosis is, theoretically, the best available therapeutic method, it may still fail in practice because of poor motivation or resistance. When resistance is not a factor, when conflicts (either conscious or unconscious) are not a hindrance, and when motivation is good, hypnosis, even with people whose hypnotic capacity is minimal, tends to be quite successful. Thus, it can be an excellent treatment for all the conditions described in the next three chapters.

6
Anxiety States

Much has been written about the "fight or flight" response. The human nervous system is designed to react automatically to threat or emergency by pouring adrenaline into the bloodstream, closing off the blood supply near the skin, interrupting digestion, and increasing vigilance. These physiological changes, which were no doubt useful in prehistoric times, are not so adaptive in modern civilization. A Neanderthal being chased by an angry animal could use the adrenaline in his bloodstream to increase his muscular activity. The same kind of flood of adrenaline, however, is not helpful to a commuter sitting caught in a traffic jam. A response that might help in the defense of a cave attacked by another tribe is not so useful in handling a critical boss.

Although a small amount of tension or anxiety can enhance performance, many people become overly anxious rather than optimally anxious. This increased anxiety produces a deterioration in ability.

For some people this anxiety will be a brief, transient irritation. For others, however, it is a chronic difficulty. Symptoms of chronic anxiety manifest themselves in various ways and can range from nervous stomach, headaches, and hives to high blood pressure, ulcerative colitis,

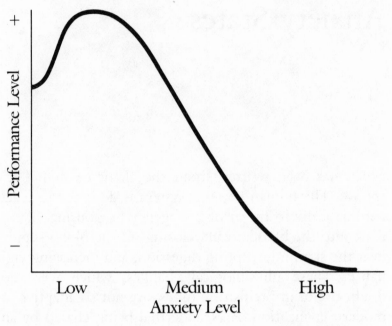

and psoriasis. Some people take their tension out on themselves, while others release it in their behavior toward others. Many people are unable to let themselves relax, even after the stress-producing situation ceases. They cannot, for example, leave the pressures of work behind when the office closes for the day.

Because of its usually relaxing nature, hypnosis is an obvious choice to deal with tension and its symptoms. The various manifestations of anxiety can be treated in ways appropriate to the particular disorder. All of these conditions share a basic strategy designed to reduce the general level of anxiety.

A useful and standard treatment method is to use an induction that includes relaxation. The hypnotized person is then instructed to "float off to a very nice place," described by the hypnotist in something like the following manner:

> *While you are feeling so comfortably relaxed, effortlessly listening to my voice, I would like you to imagine yourself floating peacefully and comfortably along. Just drift along.*
>
> *Soon you are going to find yourself arriving at a very peaceful place. Perhaps you will find yourself on a deserted beach, perhaps a lush green meadow surrounded by woods, perhaps atop a mountain surrounded by valleys. Perhaps you will find yourself in a place you know, perhaps in one that could exist only in your imagination. Wherever it is you find yourself is all right. When you reach this peaceful place, let your hand float up in the air and touch your cheek as a sign to both of us that you have arrived.*

As soon as the patient touches his or her cheek, the hypnotist proceeds with the essentials of the treatment.

> *Fine. Now, I would like you to make an association in your mind between the physical sensation of your hand touching your cheek and the physical and emotional sense of relaxation you feel. Touching your cheek is a signal that triggers relaxation. This association should be practiced every time you hypnotize yourself. This signal to relax will not only work while you are in a trance, but will serve also as a posthypnotic suggestion, helping you to relax at any time.*
>
> *Where have you found yourself to have floated?*

Given the answer of "a beach," for instance, the hypnotist goes on to develop the imagery. The patient's attention is focused on using all five senses to make the scene as vivid and real as possible.

On this beach, remember all of your senses. See the blue of the sky, look at the beach. Listen to the sound of the waves and the cries of the sea gulls. Feel the grit of the sand beneath you. Feel the warmth of the sun and the coolness of the sea breeze. Smell the fresh ocean air. That's fine. You're fully immersed in the scene, fully relaxed.

Touch your cheek once again to strengthen the association between this touch and relaxation.

Now, while your mind stays on the beach, I would like to teach you something. Please hold your hand out in front of you, up in the air, and make a tight fist. Feel the tension spread from your hand to your wrist and forearm. Your arm is stiff and tight, painfully tight. Feel the pain of the tension increase.

When you decide you don't like this tension, just reach over and touch your cheek, and as you do, you feel the sense of relaxation flood through your body. Fully relaxed, no more tightness.

From this point on, a brief series of extensions of this exercise follow: tense then relax feet, tense then relax chest and shoulders, tense then relax all muscles, and finally, feel anxious, then touch cheek and relax.

The hypnotist concludes:

You see, it is easier and more comfortable for your body to be relaxed than to be tense. Your body will naturally tend to relax if you let it. It is not work for your muscles to relax. But letting them relax can often be work for your mind. This work can be done by touching your cheek to remind you to let your muscles relax and by going to your beach scene. If, in the future, you find yourself going to some other place, that will be all right. Just remember to use all your senses to imagine a peaceful, idyllic retreat.

The patient is then instructed to practice this exercise, at least twice a day for twenty minutes at a time, and to come back in a week so that the hypnotist can see how things are going.

Frequently, such a person will return to the next session professing a great interest in continuing to use the technique, but saying that there had been no time to practice during the week. The simple complaint, "I could not find the time to practice," can be dealt with in a straightforward manner. People usually respond well to being told, "Of course a busy person like you cannot *find* time. Your schedule is so full that you must *make* time for this exercise. You must decide it is a priority and make room for it in your busy schedule."

Another common lament is that whenever the patient tries to practice, he is distracted. He is unable to concentrate no matter how hard he tries. He will report

97

that he has put in the time, but has found himself over-whelmed by extraneous thoughts and ideas. This is the kind of person who brings work along on a vacation, even on a mental one. For such a person the following suggestion would be given once he was hypnotized but before he floated off to his peaceful scene.

Now that you are feeling nicely relaxed, listening to my voice, I would like you to take a moment to let any thoughts that might be interested in getting your attention come to the surface. That's right. In a minute, you are going to let each thought which clamors for your attention have it. As you review every one, you will be able to decide whether it demands immediate action or can wait for twenty minutes. If it truly demands immediate attention, you will, of course, interrupt the hypnotic exercise, attend to the matter, and then come back to do your hypnosis later. If, however, you decide that it is nothing that cannot wait twenty minutes, you can mentally flag each idea and thought that you think is important so that it will return to you later. That's right. You need not worry about losing the idea because it will return to you at the appropriate time, when you are ready to act on it. But for now, you do not need to pay it any more attention. Now you can begin to float and drift off to your peaceful scene. As you do so, you may well find that those thoughts again try to clamor for your attention. You know, however, that there is nothing you need deal with immediately. They all can wait. There is no need even to be curious about what the thoughts are. They are interferences that are making it more difficult

*for you to do your job of floating off to a nice place. If a
thought comes along, you are not going to grab it, metaphorically, and struggle to push it out of your awareness.
To do that would be to pay attention to it. Instead, you
will let it just pass swiftly by you, saying, "I'll think of
that later." Just as the martial arts master does not block
a blow by trying to stop the punch, but rather uses the
momentum of his attacker to throw or carry the attacker
past him, so you will use the momentum of your intrud-
ing thoughts to carry them out of your awareness without even consciously acknowledging them. Now you are
ready to float off to your place. Your job is to focus all of
your conscious attention on making the scene real.*

Anxiety can manifest itself as a chronic difficulty and
appear in the form of constant low-grade tension. It can
also erupt undisguised in acute attacks or be felt as "free-
floating" anxiety. Most long-term anxieties are best
treated in psychotherapy, where the dynamic issues underlying the symptoms can be resolved. However, it is
possible to use hypnosis to take the edge off the symptoms, in much the same way as medicine can be used for
symptomatic relief.

The hypnotic approach to any anxiety is basically
the same. The patient is instructed to focus on the hypnotic induction. It is extremely difficult for an acutely
anxious person to direct attention away from his or her
anxiety and to focus it on the induction. Thus, these
patients frequently inform the hypnotist right at the start,
"I'm too nervous to become hypnotized." From the therapist's point of view, this disclaimer is really very similar

to the "I'm too busy" statement of a tense workaholic. In such cases, it is helpful for the patient to know that the hypnotist realizes he or she is asking for *very hard work*, and for the hypnotist to ask the patient to "work really hard" at concentrating. When and if this initial resistance can be overcome, the patient is instructed to "float off to a very nice place," and a standard relaxation exercise follows.

Phobias

When unreasonable anxiety, fear, or dread is experienced consistently in relation to some thing, place, or situation, it is called a phobia. Common phobias include *claustrophobia*, the fear of enclosed places, and *acrophobia*, the fear of heights, which is often confused with both *agoraphobia*, the fear of going out of one's house, and *agraphobia*, the dread of open spaces. Less common are *haematophobia*, the fear of blood, *triskaidekaphobia*, in which the number thirteen inspires panic, and *porphyrophobia*, a dread of purple.

Explanations of phobias, their causes and their cures, have been put into both psychoanalytic and behavioral terms. Within the framework of analytic theory, a phobia is understood as an expression of an unconscious conflict. Freud first described the dynamics of such a conflict in his discussion of a horse phobia suffered by "Little Hans." The young boy Hans was intensely, although unconsciously, envious of his father's relationship with his mother. Jealously wanting her all for himself, the little boy was unconsciously plagued by an urge to hurt and vanquish his rival. Hans's aggressive wish was problematic because the father whom he wished to hurt was the same father he loved.

The little boy recognized that, between his father and himself, one of the two wished to hurt the other. Because Hans could not admit that the destructive impulse was his own, he felt it must be his father who was dangerously menacing. Having then put himself in the position of needing to fear his "threatening" father, Hans found a solution that was just as intolerable as his initial aggressive impulse. He had to find a more neutral target for his fear.

The final result of this process, all of which had taken place at a level beneath his awareness, was that Hans substituted horses for his frightening father. He became horse-phobic.

Although such theoretical understanding of the origins of phobias and dynamics involved in them may be justified, the application of analytic theory does not always work well as a treatment. Making the cause of their fears conscious or known to patients often leaves them wiser but no less phobic. Once a person has experienced a phobic response over a period of time, a habit has been established.

Behavioral theory, unlike psychoanalytic theory, is built upon ideas of learned, or "conditioned," responses. For instance, Ivan Pavlov, father of behaviorism, demonstrated that a dog could be conditioned to salivate when a bell was rung. Knowing that a dog naturally salivates while eating, Pavlov rang a bell during his dog's feeding time. After frequent repetitions, the dog formed an association between the ringing sound and salivation. The animal learned *not* that the bell meant food was coming, but rather that a certain physical event (salivation) was paired with a certain cue (bell-ringing).

It is in these terms of paired or conditioned associations that behaviorists view phobias. A phobia can be taught. For instance, a child who repeatedly and simultaneously is scared by a loud noise while holding a soft, furry toy animal will not reason that the stuffed animal did not make the noise and therefore is not to be feared. Instead, the child makes an association between the toy and the experience of fear (with its concomitant physical changes of accelerated heart rate, muscle tension, flood of adrenaline) until he becomes afraid of the stuffed animal itself.

Since a phobia can be taught, it is possible to learn new responses or associations to the feared object. Behavioral treatment of phobias is derived from this idea and rests on two equally important processes. The first is reciprocal inhibition, which means that one cannot do two mutually exclusive things at the same time. One cannot, for instance, be tense and relaxed at the same instant. If a person can learn to associate relaxation with a feared object, his relaxation precludes anxiety and tension.

The second foundation of behavioral treatment is systematic desensitization, whereby a person learns, in small, manageable steps, to be less sensitive to the feared object. The child who learns to fear the stuffed animal can be cured by using such a method. First, he is comfortably seated in a large room and given a candy bar. The candy makes him feel relaxed and happy. The dreaded toy is placed in the farthest corner of the room. The fear provoked in the child by the presence of the stuffed animal at that distance is small and manageable. The pleasure of the soothing candy bar is great. Since both fear and contentment cannot coexist simultaneously, the child continues to feel at peace. With repeated similar exposures at increasingly smaller distances, the child loses his fear.

The treatment of phobias with hypnosis incorporates behavioral techniques and should also include on the part of the therapist some awareness of the possible dynamic issues involved. What is unique to hypnotic theory and treatment is the major role of trance and dissociation. A capacity for hypnotizability, operating in an unconscious and uncontrolled manner, underlies the genesis of the phobia. In hypnotic treatment the same capacity for dissociation that *caused* the phobia is made part of its cure.

A Case of Flying Phobia

Mrs. Mitchell was a twenty-nine-year-old mother of two who came to Dr. Stone seeking help for an airplane phobia. She would fly only when absolutely necessary, and then only with horrible dread. She was petrified during a flight, imagining that every variation of engine pitch, altitude, attitude, or direction presaged a fiery crash. She couldn't watch movies about planes or go to the airport to pick up arriving guests or see off departing ones. The sight of planes overhead produced panic. Even the sight of a toy airplane provoked great distress.

Outside this area of fear, she was generally cheerful and not particularly anxious or tense. Mrs. Mitchell's marriage was stable, satisfying, and happy. She enjoyed her two children.

Mrs. Mitchell was, then, a well-functioning woman with an isolated phobia. She recognized the irrational nature of her dread and was eager to rid herself of it.

As a child, Mrs. Mitchell had had no fear of airplanes and had enjoyed flying as a means of travel. Her husband had learned to fly in the military, liking it well enough to continue piloting as a hobby. During their courtship, the Mitchells had often gone up in a small plane together. In fact, Mrs. Mitchell had enjoyed this hobby so much that she began to take flying lessons herself.

Mrs. Mitchell's mother, on the other hand, was quite nervous about her daughter's flying and did not hesitate to say so, repeatedly.

When Mrs. Mitchell was twenty-five, her mother died. Mrs. Mitchell had loved her mother and was grief-stricken as she went to attend the funeral. Following the burial service, Mrs. Mitchell boarded an airplane to fly home. Taking her seat, she settled down, letting her mind drift into a somber reverie, hardly noticing when a woman sat down next to her.

This fellow traveler immediately began to talk to Mrs. Mitchell in a rather pressured way about how terrified she was of flying. Mrs. Mitchell made a few polite noises, but mostly let the woman babble as she continued to think about her mother.

The flight itself was routine and without trauma, although this woman's voice, expressing fears of imminent disaster, was a constant background throughout the trip.

Mrs. Mitchell landed safely. The minute she disembarked, however, she became overwhelmed by a feeling of great distress. She was suddenly afraid to be anywhere near airplanes. The thought of flying terrified her. At that moment she became certain that she was afraid of flying and would avoid doing so.

The crucial flight, which marked the beginning of Mrs. Mitchell's phobia, occurred in the context of grief. Mrs. Mitchell did not wish to lose her mother, and she kept her alive, metaphorically, by unconsciously assuming one of her mother's traits. That is, Mrs. Mitchell identified with her mother's nervousness about flying. A dread of planes, moreover, would interfere with Mrs. Mitchell's ability to visit her mother's grave. If she didn't visit the site, she wouldn't have to be confronted with the visible evidence of her mother's death. These kinds of psychodynamics – unconscious identification with the deceased, unconscious denial or avoidance of the reality of the death – are common in grief and are not necessarily pathological.

Mrs. Mitchell was in a special state of mind on her trip home. Her reverie, during which she was only half aware of her surroundings, can be understood as a kind of natural trance. While in this trancelike condition, she received repeated suggestions about the dangers of flight. Because she was wrapped in grief about her mother, experiencing the feelings and conflicts her loss stirred up, Mrs. Mitchell was unconsciously willing to accept her fellow traveler's version of the truth about airplanes: they are terrifying.

In the several years following the flight, Mrs. Mitchell recovered from her grief. Her feelings and conflicts resolved themselves, as is normal, over time. However, she had learned to associate the experience of extreme fear with airplanes. Thus her phobia, which developed from an unfortunate interplay of grief-related dynamic issues, a trancelike state, and fear-provoking suggestions, persisted as a kind of learned habit.

During the first treatment session, Dr. Stone told Mrs. Mitchell about the probable role of hypnotizability in phobias. Like the child with an imaginary friend, the phobic has, simultaneously, two conflicting perceptions: a horrible fear and a knowledge that there is nothing *really* to fear.

Like many phobics, Mrs. Mitchell was excited to hear the hypnotic theory. When Dr. Stone described how an unconscious suggestion had produced a realistic experience of disaster that was too strong to ignore, she responded, "Yes, that's exactly how it feels. No one has ever understood just how real it feels." The vividly imagined disaster felt as real to her as the actual situation.

Dr. Stone told her he would teach her a constructive use of her capacity for trance. Instead of passively slipping into a hypnotic state regulated by her unconscious, Mrs. Mitchell would learn conscious control of hypnosis.

As a second stage of treatment, she would be taught how to get into a state that would allow her to travel by plane in a relaxed, though passive way. Finally, she would learn to fear airplanes no longer.

Having outlined the course of the next sessions, Dr. Stone taught Mrs. Mitchell to hypnotize herself. She left with instructions to practice at home at least twice a day so that she would become confident in her ability to enter the state at will.

When she returned the following week, Mrs. Mitchell reported that she had practiced regularly, although several times she had fallen asleep while using hypnosis. It was a sign of good motivation and prognosis that she practiced so regularly. (Patients with poor motivation, or with good motivation to change but unresolved unconscious conflicts, often do not practice, although they frequently have very good excuses for not doing so.)

Dr. Stone told Mrs. Mitchell that he thought they could use hypnosis successfully to treat her phobia and that it typically took six to eight sessions to cure such a problem. Although the number of sessions could vary quite a bit from one person to the next, he would remain available for the duration.

He explained to Mrs. Mitchell that she could do the exercise he was about to teach her if she were to board a plane that same day. This exercise is akin to taking a tranquilizer or a drink before boarding. The fear continues to exist, but it can be mastered temporarily. The exercise ensures that one will be left confident that flight is possible, although one must still work to control the anxiety. (It is not at all unusual for patients to delay seeking help until just before they are due to fly. In such cases, the therapist may have only two sessions in which to work and needs a quick, if incomplete, method of dealing with the anxiety.)

Dr. Stone therefore proceeded with an induction and suggestions that Mrs. Mitchell "float off to a very nice place." As in the treatment of less specific anxiety, once at this idyllic retreat (a beach), Mrs. Mitchell was taught the tense and relax exercise. Dr. Stone then continued, saying:

> *Now that you know how to go to this special place, you realize that you could do so at any time. You have learned to establish an internal, tranquil reality that seems more real in some ways than your external environment. You could do this outside of my office as well as in it. You could do it at home, on a train, or any place where your active participation and mental attention are not needed.*
>
> *One place you could do this exercise is aboard an airplane. While you stay peacefully at your very nice place, relaxed and listening to my voice, I am going to mention a few points to you. While on an airplane, there is nothing you need do. If you were sound asleep, the flight would continue just as though you were awake. In a way, the airplane is a machine for transporting your body from one place to another. Your mind is only along accompanying your body. If your mind were to be at some other, more pleasant place, your body could be transported just as well. In fact, your body is negatively affected if your mind is anxious and producing tension.*

Because of this, you can comfortably fly by putting your-self into this relaxed hypnotic state.

The rational decision to fly or not to fly is one that everyone makes for him or herself. Many people choose to fly because statistically it is a safer form of travel than driving. If you choose not to fly, that would be all right. The fact that you are here indicates that you have de-cided to fly and wish to fly, but find it hard to do so. You know that the time to decide whether or not you wish to fly is when you make your travel plans, not when you are aboard the airplane.

As we have discussed, the problem has been that while your body has safely flown, your mind has been busily producing and responding to imagined scenes of disaster. When you say, "That is not real," you have had the problem that it feels real. When you have ordered yourself, "Don't think about the plane crashing," the or-der itself brought the frightening image to mind. Say-ing, "Don't think about the number four," puts that number into your attention. However, saying, "Concen-trate on the letter J," and doing so, has the effect of mak-ing you not think of the number four.

Whenever you wish to fly, you can do so easily and comfortably by choosing to send your body by air while your mind is pleasantly relaxing on a beach or other nice place.

Just relax now and focus all your concentration on being on the beach. While you concentrate so deeply on experiencing the beach, you realize that it would not matter if your body were aboard a plane. In fact, you could imagine, if you wished, that we were aboard an

*airplane rather than in my office, while you focus on
your beach scene. You see—your muscles and mind are so
relaxed that there is no room for tension.*

*You will be able to achieve this state whenever you
need or wish to do so. Simply follow the method we used
today.*

*It requires work and concentration to focus on your
scene rather than to be distracted by the milieu of an airplane, but you can do it.*

*You may be so relaxed that you drift off to sleep. If
that happens, it will be all right.*

*You may be so relaxed and calm that you realize
you need fear nothing, and you wish to look around. If
that is comfortable, you may.*

*Just remember to travel to the airport in a light
trance, not letting yourself imagine the flight, only the
idyllic scene. When you board the plane and reach your
seat, rehypnotize yourself and enter a deeper trance for
travel.*

Dr. Stone told Mrs. Mitchell that she now knew that
she could fly without fear. In their next sessions, he
would help her go about the task of learning new, comfortable associations with planes.

The method used for the rest of Mrs. Mitchell's
treatment is a derivation of systematic desensitization.
To do a classical systematic desensitization, the therapist
develops with the patient a hierarchy of anxiety-arousing
experiences, graded from the least frightening to the
most terrifying. While the patient relaxes, it is suggested
that he vividly imagine himself to be in the first (least

threatening) situation of the hierarchy. If the patient signals anxiety, the therapist *immediately* returns him to the relaxed state.

When the patient can tolerate a mildly feared situation without anxiety, the therapist goes on to the next situation in the hierarchy, one a little more frightening. This technique is rather like successively removing the bottom card from a deck of playing cards. As each is removed, all the others drop a bit until each in turn is the bottom.

If each situation in the hierarchy were presented in fantasy, the procedure would be called an *imaginal* desensitization. If the patient in fact is exposed to the feared situation or thing, an *in vivo* desensitization is being used. Both work equally well, for it is not the actual realistic danger that is feared but what it represents to the patient's mind.

When Mrs. Mitchell returned for her next appointment, she reported that again she had practiced regularly and felt confident in her ability to fly with the help of hypnosis.

Dr. Stone congratulated her, then induced trance. Again she was instructed to go to her peaceful beach scene. He reemphasized her ability to stay relaxed while flying, adding that she wanted not only to fly despite her fear but to overcome her fear. For that purpose, he was going to suggest to her a number of different scenes that she was to imagine vividly.

As I present each scene, let yourself peacefully and comfortably imagine it. Do not make the mistake of antici-

pating and jumping ahead. For example, if I say imagine yourself driving to the beach, do not imagine yourself swimming. Just imagine being in the car and driving along the road that leads to the beach.

If at any point you begin to feel tense, reach up and touch your cheek. Doing so will remind your muscles to relax and will signal me that you were experiencing some anxiety.

Now imagine that you were anticipating some time off from work. Imagine an upcoming vacation. Imagine talking over with your husband where you might go; choose a place you would like to visit. You realize you will be able to go only if you fly there, but for now you are only thinking of the vacation.

Now imagine going to the phone to call the airline for a reservation. You are not on the plane, simply making a phone call. Make the reservation. That's fine. Just a phone call, no planes now.

Imagine it is six weeks before you leave. When you think of it, you know it is in the future, not the present, and that you have learned a skill that overcomes panic. Time passes. You are at home, comfortable and relaxed, and realize it is one month until you go. More time passes. . . . It is three weeks till you fly . . . two weeks . . . one week.

Mrs. Mitchell touched her cheek, and Dr. Stone knew she was experiencing some tension. He asked her to imagine her peaceful beach scene. When she was fully relaxed, he suggested that she imagine again that it was two weeks before her flight. (When a patient signals anxiety, the therapist orders an immediate return to the peaceful place. Once calm is complete, the *previous,* already tolerated scene can be slowly reintroduced. Calmness and mastery are stressed, and intervening scenes are added if it seems necessary.)

They then proceeded slowly through the passage of days, and Mrs. Mitchell was able to remain relaxed. Dr. Stone suggested,

> *Imagine that your ticket arrives in the mail. You are not afraid of a piece of paper. You are glad it is here.*
>
> *It is the day before you are to leave. You are at home, comfortable and relaxed. You peacefully begin to prepare for tomorrow. Get out your suitcase now and begin to pack. Get everything ready. All packed. Time to go to sleep now. Nicely relaxed.*

Since their time was up, Dr. Stone ended trance, and they arranged to continue this work at the next session.

When Mrs. Mitchell returned, they reviewed the previously imagined scenes, then moved on to the day of her trip.

> *Now you wake up, and the first thing you do is to go through the exercise of getting yourself nicely relaxed. You can keep this feeling all day, strengthening it as needed. You know in the past you had this sort of dissociative experience and inadvertently followed some painful suggestions. Today, if that should begin to happen, you will recognize this for what it is and ignore or override it.*

Now it's an hour before you leave the house. Time moves by . . . half an hour to go . . . fifteen minutes. It is time to load up the car and leave. Get your suitcase. Now get in the car.

Drive away from the house, through the familiar streets of the neighborhood, then onto the highway. Continue on the highway, nice and relaxed. Now turn off for the airport tunnel. Follow the signs to the departure areas. Stop the car; unload your bags. Enter the terminal. Fine. Now go to the check-in area, give the attendant your luggage for loading, and choose your seat. You are told your gate number, so you begin to walk toward it. Stop at the security area, and pass through the metal detector. Good. Now walk down the corridor to your gate.

At the gate you feel so proud of yourself for being in control, knowing you are master of your suggestions and of your experiences. You check in, take a seat in the waiting area, close your eyes, and briefly repeat your exercise. That's right. Enter the trance more deeply, become fully relaxed. Now, staying very relaxed, you almost leave the trance but remain slightly hypnotized. Good. The loudspeaker announces that your flight is ready for boarding, so you open your eyes, get up, and walk comfortably over to the door. Now walk through the tunnel and enter the airplane.

Because Mrs. Mitchell, like so many other airplane phobics, had rated takeoff as extremely distressing, Dr. Stone did not suggest she imagine this scene next. Instead, he proceeded to the landing.

You are on the plane, and the captain's voice comes over the intercom. He announces, "We are beginning our final descent for landing. We are right on time, and conditions are fine."

You fasten your seat belt and watch as the plane gets ready to land. Peaceful and relaxed. Hear the engine noises change, as they should. Feel the plane drop. Feel your ears pop as the altitude decreases. Soon you will be there on the ground and at your destination. That's right, feel the plane descend. Now you feel the bump as the wheels touch the runway. Now hear the roar of the air brakes as the engines slow the plane. Feel yourself push forward in your seat as the plane slows. Now you are rolling slowly along the runway, now along the plane's route to the gate. You are in the arrival lounge, ready to get your luggage. You feel great. Pleased and successful.

Mrs. Mitchell was learning very well to pair her relaxed state with imagined plane scenes. They scheduled another appointment for the following week, agreeing that it would probably be her last.

In this fifth session, Dr. Stone led Mrs. Mitchell to imagine the landing scene once again, then continued, suggesting the most frightening aspect of flying.

As you walk down the corridor to the luggage carousel, your mind drifts back. Let your mind go back to when you were so comfortably seated on the plane. You are eating your in-flight meal on the plane. Relaxed, eating your meal, flying right along. A little bored, perhaps, eager to arrive at your destination, but glad to be getting there so quickly and comfortably.

Now the flight attendant leaves, and you settle back and relax. Let your mind go back to the way you felt when the plane first began to move, coasting slowly away from the airport.

Nicely relaxed, you sit back in your seat, excited to be on the way. Feel the plane rolling across the tarmac to the runway, waiting in line to take off.

Now, at the beginning of the runway, you relax and listen to the engine revving up. They do all the work—you don't have to do it for them. Relax, settle back, let the engines work, making a loud noise. That's a good sign that they are working well. Now the brakes are released, and with comfortable excitement, you feel the surge of power as the plane picks up speed, faster and faster, till the bump of the landing gear leaving the ground lets you know you are airborne.

Relax and feel the plane climb higher and higher to its safe cruising altitude. Feel your ears pop. Fine. You've taken off. You're flying.

Now you are back at your destination. Here comes your suitcase. Pick it up and leave the airport, proud of yourself and the way you flew comfortably, like the non-phobic person you are.

Out of trance, Dr. Stone told Mrs. Mitchell again that she really was cured of her phobia. Because solid new learning had taken place through an imaginal desensitization, she now associated planes with relaxation instead of with anxiety. Having rid herself of her phobia, she need not hypnotize herself again. Both Dr. Stone and Mrs. Mitchell agreed, however, that she could derive added confidence from knowing that if she ever began to create a phobia again, she had a method for dealing with it. She now knew how to take charge of trance rather than having it take charge of her.

Mrs. Mitchell agreed to let Dr. Stone know how she was doing within the next several months, and they concluded a successful treatment at this point. Mrs. Mitchell phoned one month later to report that she had taken a shuttle flight with pleasure, not anxiety.

Additional Techniques for Treating Flying Phobias

A variety of treatment methods may be substituted for or used in addition to those already mentioned. Briefly, these methods are as follows:

1. For patients who have agoraphobic tendencies, the therapist may make the first imagined flight the return trip, the trip that brings the person home.

2. Relaxation during the first session can be enhanced by the Tense and Relax method.

3. The therapist might suggest that the patient imagine himself as very light—so light, in fact, that he is floating inside the airplane, rather like a helium balloon. He might be so light that he would stay aloft even if the plane crashed. His buoyancy might be so great that he

could even keep the plane airborne by himself, as a hot-air balloon supports the basket.

4. A focus on the destination can be helpful for many people. For example, a patient might be leaving a winter climate for a vacation in the sun. He could be instructed to imagine the door to the airport as the entrance to his destination. That is, the door to New York's La Guardia Airport might be seen as the entrance to sunny San Diego. Arriving at the airport might be experienced as going to the beach, and all aspects of the plane trip itself would be perceived as part of the beach trip. The patient can feel relieved and relaxed at the sense of already being there.

5. It is possible to enhance a sense of dissociation by creating a new reality. One might, for example, imagine that the airport is really the entrance to the Disneyland "Airplane" ride. The illusion might be that the whole "flight," designed with a very careful eye toward accurate and realistic detail, is nothing more than a special-effects project. A person could imagine, on a real plane, that what he sees are only such effects.

Agoraphobia

There are phobias that, in both their persistence and their cure, are more complex than the airplane phobia just described. These more complicated phobias do not develop from conditioned response but are the result of ongoing unconscious conflict. While the best-known treatment for phobias that are habits is hypnotically enhanced behavior modification, psychodynamically based phobias require psychotherapy. Hypnosis in such cases is used to take the edge off the symptoms.

A person with a fear of heights, for instance, often possesses a strong, although unconscious, atavistic wish to fly like a bird. When high up, he is afraid he will forget what he really knows (that he can't fly) and will hurl himself down. The phobia is an extreme measure taken to remind him not to launch himself. The treatment of this phobia would consist of (1) making conscious the wish to fly and (2) making suggestions designed to strengthen awareness of the inability to fly. The person would then stay aware of a mild but adequate caution against jumping and so need not use the "overkill" of the phobia.

Like the fear of heights, agoraphobia is one of the more complex phobias. This condition, more frequently experienced by women than by men, is a fear of going out in public. The affected individual becomes extremely anxious when leaving the house. Driving, particularly when alone, is often difficult. Routine tasks such as shopping may become totally impossible. Some victims become literally housebound, not stepping out of the front door for years.

When someone with agoraphobia asks for help, a combination of direct, symptomatic treatment and long-term treatment of the underlying conflict are both necessary. The symptom must be sufficiently relieved for the phobic individual to be able to go out of the house and reach the therapist's office. If, however, the underlying problem, the cause of the fear, is ignored, the phobia or substitute symptoms will persist.

A Case of Agoraphobia

Mrs. Barrett was a forty-two-year-old mother of three. She was brought to Dr. Browning's office by her older sister, Mrs. McCormick, because she had been increasingly unable to leave her home. The Barretts occupied half of a two-family house, the McCormicks living in the other half. Mr. Barrett was a factory worker who was quite impatient with his wife's "silliness." Mrs. Barrett's mother was a widow who, since the death of her husband, had become heavily dependent on her daughter. Although she lived one-half hour's drive away, she would feel, for instance, quite comfortable demanding that Mrs. Barrett drop whatever she was doing and come over to escort her around the corner for a loaf of bread.

Mrs. Barrett had always been a homebody. She had never worked to support herself and had never lived on her own. She married Mr. Barrett right after her high school graduation and had moved straight from her parents' house into her present home. Although there had been little cause for her to go out much, Mrs. Barrett had never experienced difficulty doing so until her mother was widowed, three years before. Since that time she had begun limiting the number of places she would go. As her anxiety grew, the distance she would travel shrank. She could go farther with companions than alone. It was easier for her to take necessary trips (e.g., taking the children to the orthodontist) than pleasurable ones, such as shopping. Typically it was less difficult for her to travel back to her house than to travel away from it.

In the first session, Dr. Browning proposed a course of treatment. She suggested a psychiatric evaluation of Mrs. Barrett's problem. Then she would proceed to teach her self-hypnosis and how to use it for symptom relief. Once Mrs. Barrett experienced enough relief to allow her to function, they would go on to more traditional, insight-oriented psychotherapy. Mrs. Barrett said that she was not sure about the therapy part because she was not "crazy," but she did want to start the hypnosis. Dr. Browning agreed.

After a consequently brief evaluation, Dr. Browning taught Mrs. Barrett self-hypnosis and began to work on her phobia. The first step for Mrs. Barrett was learning to relax and to tolerate being a passenger in a car, just as an airplane phobic would first learn to manage a flight. A standard desensitization then followed, beginning with Mrs. Barrett walking out the front door to get her newspaper and coming right back. The deconditioning moved through sitting in the car while it was parked in the driveway, to riding comfortably in the passenger seat while her mind went to some pleasant place, and eventually to driving around the block.

Mrs. Barrett seemed to make excellent progress during her first two sessions. For a variety of reasons, however, she often was unable to practice regularly between appointment times. This inconsistency, she insisted, was not due to lack of motivation. Dr. Browning did not argue the point, as she felt it would be futile to do so. Mrs. Barrett did manage to practice well following this appointment.

When she came to the fourth session, however, Mrs. Barrett was quite upset. "I've been practicing just like you taught me, but when Sis and I went to visit my mother, something happened." What had happened was that as Mrs. Barrett stepped out the front door, her vision became so blurred that she could not see the stairs well enough to walk down them. This blurred vision remained for several hours after she went back into her house and lay down. Needless to say, the session was devoted to the treatment of Mrs. Barrett's new conversion symptom.

Because her patient wasn't ready for a psychodynamic interpretation of her symptom, Dr. Browning did not point out that Mrs. Barrett might have some mixed feelings about visiting her demanding mother. Instead, the doctor taught her, in trance, how to blur her vision deliberately. Mrs. Barrett discovered that if she stared at a certain spot long enough, it began to look fuzzy. She learned to refocus her eyes, changing at will from blurry to clear sight. Mrs. Barrett left the hour believing she could handle the blindness should it reoccur.

The next week, however, she once again was very distressed. She had had no further trouble with her vision, but when she went to drive her car, she found she had lost all sensation in her legs. Because of this numbness, she could not feel the pedals well enough to drive. In fact, when she walked back into her house, it was on legs that felt like "dead meat." This symptom had continued all week with no interruption.

Once again, the hour focused on dealing with this new problem. Dr. Browning's approach consisted of pointing out how Mrs. Barrett could produce this condition intentionally by using hypnosis. Teaching her to end as well as to initiate the symptom was intended to give Mrs. Barrett a sense of increased control and decreased fear. Additionally, Dr. Browning introduced a psychodynamic (partial) interpretation of the events of her patient's week. "On the one hand," she suggested, "you very much wanted to go out, but on the other, you were frightened to do so. The numbness in your legs solved the problem by making it impossible to go out no matter how much you wanted to." Dr. Browning did not challenge Mrs. Barrett's perception that she wholeheartedly wanted to go out and did not discuss the reasons why she feared doing so. She left the session feeling in control over the numbness and resolved to continue working on her agoraphobia.

In the following four weeks, Mrs. Barrett continued to develop new symptoms as quickly as she could be cured of the old ones. One by one, she was afflicted with severe headaches, a sense of depersonalization, hoarseness in her throat that became so bad that she couldn't speak outside of the house, and a fainting attack. Finally, she began a session by saying she had had no new symptoms during the week. She had, however, experienced a fearful reluctance to leave the house. "I went out anyway," she related, "but when I got to the card shop, I got so scared, I couldn't buy anything." Mrs. Barrett had been overwhelmed by panic so strong she was forced to leave the store. "Well," she said to Dr. Browning, "I guess maybe there is something going on that is making me so afraid to go out. It seems like every time we cure one thing, another pops up. I guess maybe we do need to talk about what else is going on in my life, like you said." Dr. Browning concurred, and they agreed to begin a course of traditional, insight-oriented psychotherapy.

When Dr. Browning suggested they might use hypnosis to help Mrs. Barrett overcome her panic reaction to the card shop, she said, "No, we'd better not. Let's use hypnosis to let me leave the house for anyplace else, but I'll stay afraid of that store. I know me. If it gets hard to talk about things, I'm going to want to stop. And if I do, I know now, I'll get worse again. I don't really need to go to that store anyway, and this way, I'll have a reminder to myself, like a warning – if I don't keep coming here until I've fixed what's behind all this, the card shop is how I'll feel all the time."

Early in the course of psychotherapy, it became clear that a major dilemma for Mrs. Barrett was how to deal with her angry feelings. It was particularly difficult for her to let herself feel anger toward people she cared about, especially her mother and husband. Therefore, two sessions were devoted to hypnotic treatment of this issue. In the first of these two hours, Dr. Browning said:

As we have discussed in therapy, you have trouble letting yourself know just how angry you sometimes get. It is as though you are afraid your anger could kill someone. We know that you are not really Lizzy Borden, but a part of you tries to control you as if you were. We know that those controls should be loosened, that then you would just be a little angry like most normal people. Let's help you learn to do that.

Remember the other day when your mother told you your spaghetti was overcooked and that your lettuce was old and tough? Good. Now imagine yourself in a boxing ring with her. The referee will keep things from getting out of hand, so you don't need to control yourself. As a fighter your job is to fight. The bell rings, you run out, and sock her. Pow. Right in the kisser. Whack her again. Pow. The scene takes on a cartoon quality. Pick up a big rock and smash it on her head. Crunch. Just like Wily Coyote. Give her a stick of dynamite. Kabooom! And here she comes back for more. Give her the old one-two. Hit her with a rubber chicken. Dump a bowl of spaghetti over her head. That's right. It's getting rather funny now. Look at the noodles drip over her ears. That'll teach her to say, "I think you overcooked it, dear." Tell her next time you'll use a frozen leg of lamb and that you'll eat the murder weapon.

As you engage in this combat, continuing to give her a whack every few minutes to keep her in line, you realize that you haven't really killed her. Also, you realize that you feel better. Imagining letting your anger out makes you feel better and does not really hurt her. In fact, the two of you get along better now.

What Dr. Browning suggested to Mrs. Barrett in hypnosis was not essentially different than what they had been discussing in their traditional psychotherapy sessions. Rather than saying, "You must have been angry," or "You are afraid that your anger will kill your mother, but it really will not," Dr. Browning gave these same messages through the medium of vivid imagery. What was helpful about using hypnosis was that Mrs. Barrett could vividly imagine, and thus "practice," the expression of anger as not dangerous or deadly.

In their next session, Dr. Browning continued:

> *Now that the image of you as a potential murderess has been put in its proper perspective, let's go back to this last time your mother criticized your cooking. Go back into the past and feel yourself once again there with her. Hear the criticism. Realize that the feeling you are experiencing is a fear of being angry, and realize you need not fear your anger. That's right. You're mad. You know you will feel better and get along with her better if you do not bottle up the feeling. What could you say that would let out your angry feelings in a constructive way?*

At this point Mrs. Barrett and Dr. Browning began working out strategies for dealing with the situation and running through them in trance. Mrs. Barrett continued to work well in treatment after her initial rocky start. From time to time, hypnosis was used to help her overcome brief, transient phobic episodes. These always occurred at stressful periods in the treatment. She also learned to use self-hypnosis to deal with her less crippling anxieties. Her very successful course of treatment lasted several years.

126

Performance Anxiety

Some fears, which may or may not reach phobic propor-
tions, occur in relation to the performance of a certain
action or activity. When the degree of distress involved
is not great enough to warrant the name of "phobia,"
the fear is merely called a "performance anxiety." This
sort of anxiety arises in countless situations. The actions
of singing or playing a musical instrument, appearing in
a play, or starring in an athletic contest also often provoke
fear. Similarly, though less publicly, performance anxiety
can occur when one takes an exam, goes for a job inter-
view, or has a sexual encounter.

Some strategies involved in treating performance
anxieties are similar to those used to treat phobias. A
systematic desensitization is often integral to the cure in
both cases. However, the hypnotic techniques useful for
non-action-oriented anxieties (e.g., riding in an airplane)
are not helpful when the fear is of *doing* something (piloting an airplane). One cannot, for instance, simply relax,
sit back, and detach one's mind from one's body while
lecturing, driving a car, or playing in a tennis tourna-
ment. The activity required precludes such a passive
stance.

In general, the basic principles used to treat one
performance anxiety apply to others as well.

Fear of Public Speaking

One of the most common of all performance anxieties is
public speaking. Most people are awed by crowds and

are quite hesitant to appear before an audience. Distress about public speaking includes not only delivering a prepared speech but also talking extemporaneously or simply asking a question. The degree of difficulty speaking in public ranges from the need for an extra "gulp" before beginning a talk, to extreme impairment or even total inability to speak: a student takes a leave of absence from medical school because she cannot present cases to instructors; a businessman's career is circumscribed by his reluctance to accept a promotion that would require public talks; a would-be lawyer turns down an offer from a good law school because he cannot speak in class. It is this kind of extreme difficulty in speaking that most often motivates patients to ask for hypnotic treatment.

A Case of Anxiety in Public Speaking

Mr. Dow, a twenty-five-year-old graduate student in architecture, was referred to the hospital hypnosis clinic by his professor because he had difficulty presenting in seminars. He was seen there by a staff social worker, Ms. Russell, who was experienced in the therapeutic use of hypnosis.

In the initial evaluation, Mr. Dow was found to be a pleasant and intelligent young man who was very strongly motivated toward professional success. His general level of functioning was quite good, and there was no evidence of severe psychological disturbance. He had some obvious areas of unresolved conflict but had no wish to work on them in therapy at this time.

As he saw it, Mr. Dow's problem was that he could not easily speak in class. He had coped with this lifelong difficulty by avoidance – for example, he took only large lecture classes in college. Avoidance was no longer an option because his professional training required seminars. Furthermore, both classes and eventual career demanded that he verbally present proposals to prospective clients.

The most difficult kind of talking for Mr. Dow was a formal presentation of prepared material. He found it moderately difficult to speak spontaneously in class, but it became easier once he had warmed up. Trivial talk, such as having people at a table introduce themselves, was inordinately difficult for him, and the longer he had to wait his turn to speak, the more difficult it became.

In the first treatment session, Ms. Russell induced hypnosis and found Mr. Dow to be quite responsive. It was suggested to him that he float to a very nice place where he would be safe and relaxed. He chose a meadow. Once there, he was told to touch his cheek and make an association between the sensation of this touch and the feeling of peace and relaxation.

"While you are feeling so relaxed in this meadow," said Ms. Russell, "I would like you to imagine that you have thought up a brief presentation on a subject you enjoy. Perhaps you might think of speaking about a pleasant evening you have had or where you spent last weekend. If you should become at all tense, touch your cheek. This will relax you and signal to me that you are tense."

First Ms. Russell had Mr. Dow imagine saying his presentation while alone in the meadow. Then she in-

structed him to do this a second time. When he had done
so, she said,

> *You didn't notice, but your best friend came up behind*
> *you and was listening all the while you were speaking.*
> *Feel the pride as he tells you what a nice speech you gave.*
> *As you think about this, you realize that the difficulty is*
> *not that you cannot speak before an audience, but rather*
> *that you have been stopping yourself. To speak before*
> *your friend is the same as speaking alone.*
>
> > *Now, making sure there is no one there but you and*
> *your friend, repeat the speech. You see – it was no more*
> *difficult than when you were alone. Now do it again*
> *with your friend. You guessed it. Three more friends*
> *overheard.*

Having graphically demonstrated that the basic task
of speaking occurred regardless of the presence or absence of an audience, Ms. Russell proceeded to do a
standard desensitization.

In subsequent sessions she went on to teach Mr.
Dow a number of additional techniques. First she enhanced his sense of control over his voice.

> *Imagine a dial in your mind. Reach out and twist the*
> *dial; move it back and forth along the various settings.*
> *It is a volume control. In a moment I would like you to*
> *say, "Aaaaaaaaaaaaaaa," and as you do, twist the vol-*
> *ume control. You will begin very softly and become quite*
> *loud as you progress. Do it now.*

Mr. Dow complied nicely. Ms. Russell then stated,

You have worried that your voice will be too soft to be heard. See how you can control the volume.

As Mr. Dow continued to work on this exercise, he began to feel less worried about his voice.

It is a very common experience, when one is anxious, to become aware of one's rapid breathing and racing heartbeat. Often this awareness generates even more anxiety. In the next session, therefore, Ms. Russell told Mr. Dow:

You have described how your breathing has been strained and your heart has seemed to pound before you speak. Let's work on that. While you are so relaxed, I would like you to focus your attention inward. Feel your heartbeat. You see – it is easy to do. Awareness of your heart's beat merely means that you are focusing your attention inside rather than outside. In the past, you have not liked seeing an audience. You tried to avoid seeing it by focusing within yourself. When you became aware of your heart, you worried that this meant it was beating too hard. Continue to focus on your heartbeat until you get bored with it. It really is dull and repetitive. When you get bored, stop paying attention to it. You know as long as it is beating you are fine. There is no need to monitor it. It will continue to beat on its own. If you notice your heartbeat, you will know it only means you are looking there. When it gets boring, you can look elsewhere.

Now, imagine you are running in a race. As you race, your lungs strain to bring oxygen to your muscles. Your heart beats quickly to carry the oxygen through your body. There, you have done it. You have crossed the finish line. You won! Collapse on the grass and regain your breath. Feel your heart and lungs slow down. See, you can slow them. If you find your heart and lungs speeding up before you speak, watch yourself break the tape and win the race. As soon as the race is won, your body can slow down and relax.

Ms. Russell also taught Mr. Dow a variety of other exercises. One was to imagine a strong positive response at the conclusion of his talk. The sense of a positive outcome helped him to approach the experience without the dread of potential humiliation. Another exercise was to imagine the audience in a variety of undignified positions. On one occasion they were dressed in clown suits. On another they were all five-year-olds. On another they were all naked. None of these groups was very frightening. (A variation of this approach was to negatively hallucinate the entire audience and experience himself presenting to an empty room.

Mr. Dow reported a great deal of relief after the eighth and final session.

Two years later he came again to the clinic. At that time he reported that he had continued to have no difficulty speaking in public but was having a problem dealing with co-workers. He was then referred for traditional psychotherapy.

If the speaking difficulty came on at a particular time, or if the patient is interested in approaching the problem more dynamically, one additional hypnotic technique is often useful. The focus of this final method is an age regression to the time the fear was first felt. Having heard about the initial traumatic experience, the therapist tries to find out what made it so frightening. He then tries to modify the memory. A typical approach would be to have the patient imagine a trusted, loving parent, some other adult who is caring, or even the patient himself as a grownup help the child through the frightening experience.

In Summary

The hypnotic treatment of any kind of anxiety, whether unfocused, phobic, or performance-related, most often includes, as one strategy, a relaxation exercise. The theory behind this practice is *reciprocal inhibition*. A person cannot be relaxed and anxious at the same time. Anxiety learned through paired associations yields when new, tension-free responses are learned. Systematic desensitization is also often crucial in the treatment of phobic and/or performance anxiety. Hypnosis makes it possible to experience each component of an anxiety-arousing hierarchy and at the same time to "practice" the necessary relaxed responses. When a capacity for hypnotizability has been a major contributing factor in the formation of a fear, as seems to be the case with phobias, a *controlled* use of trance can be highly effective in curing it.

Generalized tension, performance anxieties, or phobias that persist on the basis of psychodynamic conflict are most often best helped by psychotherapy. Within the context of such thereapy, hypnosis can be used to strengthen, by means of graphic imagery, the emotional impact of an interpretation or insight that might otherwise remain purely intellectual. Additionally, given information about the root of a fear, therapist and patient can use trance to replace the original scenes with new, consciously edited screen memories. Such artificial memories make the original trauma less fearful. Finally, as a means of catharsis, hypnosis is useful in lowering the intensity or amount of energy a fear has. Thus the fear becomes less highly charged and not of phobic proportion.

7
Hysterical Symptoms

The word "hysterical" can refer both to a neurosis and to certain kinds of symptoms. The first is a psychiatric diagnosis, the second are the manifest signs of underlying conflict. A hysterical neurotic would be defined, in psychoanalytic terms, as one whose reality testing was intact, whose unconscious conflicts were at the Oedipal level of psychosexual development, and whose major defense mechanism was repression (the means by which intolerable desires and memories are kept out of conscious awareness). The hysterical symptoms – dissociation, amnesia, conversion reaction, and multiple personality – arise, in part, from an overuse of repression. However, this overuse is *not* confined to people who could be diagnosed as "hysterical neurotics." Hysterical symptoms can also develop in normal people and in people whose psychopathology is nonhysterical (obsessives, borderlines, etc.).

Although both Charcot and Janet believed that only hysterics could be hypnotized and that hypnotizability was linked to diagnosis, most modern theorists hold that trance potential exists regardless of the diagnosis of hysterical neurosis. A majority of these theorists would agree, however, that hysterical *symptoms* are related to the capacity for hypnotizability.

Amnesia

Amnesia is a hysterical symptom, yet one need not be neurotic to develop memory loss. In fact, a great many people routinely develop small bursts of amnesia when it comes to remembering appointments, names, or the whereabouts of misplaced items. Often, memory loss occurs when the individual is in a trancelike, semidissociative state. When, for example, one is dreamily looking forward to a pleasant event, brooding over a fight, or feeling sad, attention is partially removed from whatever action one happens to be performing at the time. Because it was not the object of full attention, that action tends to be easy to forget.

A Case of Mild Amnesia

Mrs. Brody, an antique dealer, came to consult with Dr. Cleaves to help her find a missing brooch, part of some new inventory. She described having seen it the previous week. She knew she had hidden the brooch right before closing the shop for the night, but the next morning could not remember where she had put it.

In hypnosis Mrs. Brody was directed to remember the day she had lost the brooch, but was told *not* to try consciously to remember where she had put it. After all, Dr. Cleaves pointed out, if she were able to remember where this bit of jewelry was by sheer effort, she would have done so already and saved herself a trip to the hypnotist.

As with all tip-of-the-tongue phenomena, the path to memory is cleared by *not* focusing on the thing to be recalled. Memory, it seems, is not organized alphabetically, numerically, or chronologically. Instead, Dr. Cleaves explained, it is grouped by feeling state. When an individual feels good or bad, happy or sad, he is likely to be able to recall easily other times when he felt that same way. Therefore, Mrs. Brody was to direct all of her attention to her *mood* as it was on the day in question.

Focusing on how she felt, she remembered that she was quite excited about a party she was going to that evening. Mrs. Brody described walking around the shop, happily dreaming about the pleasant evening she anticipated. Suddenly, she said, "That's it! I wrapped it in a piece of tissue paper and stuck it inside the cigar box."

The Mood-Tracking Technique in Therapy

Sometimes this mood-tracking technique can be useful in traditional psychotherapy. For example, an elementary school teacher had an inordinate amount of difficulty insisting on good student behavior. He found it impossible to figure out why this particular part of his job was so conflictual for him. One day, as he angrily tried to correct a student, he noticed that the muscles in his arms held them rigid. He then realized that his arms always stiffened in this kind of situation.

In his next therapy session, he was hypnotized and told to focus on feeling that same tension in his arms.

He was directed to go back to the most recent experience of feeling this rigidity, to feel it becoming stronger, and then to let his mind freely travel through time and space. When he did so, he quickly came up with a vivid memory of his mother furiously hitting him. He was thus "disciplined" for talking to a classmate instead of listening attentively to his second-grade teacher. He then realized that every time he reprimanded a student, he was reliving that old traumatic event, trying at the same time to maintain more self-control than his mother had had.

A Case of Long-term Amnesia

Mr. Frank had a major amnesia for which his therapist referred him to Mrs. Gray, a clinical social worker trained in the use of hypnosis. A forty-five-year-old widower, Mr. Frank remembered *nothing* about his eighteen years of marriage. He did not dispute the fact that he had been married, and if someone mentioned an event that had taken place during his marriage, he could intellectually know that it must have happened, but he had no sense of having lived through it.

When Mrs. Gray hypnotized him, she suggested that he imagine himself at the time of his wife's death. Mr. Frank was unable to do so, saying he had no memory of it. He was then told to go back to just before he met his wife. This he could do because the earlier period of life was not blanketed by the amnesia surrounding his marriage. Mr. Frank was able to proceed to the time he met and married his wife. As is typical in amnesia, the block to memory was strong against a direct assault but relatively weak against a "back door" approach. He then became extremely sad and was able to go ahead to her death. The death became quite vivid, and he recalled feeling very angry at her for deserting him. Mr. Frank had been so unable to face his anger at his wife that he had been compelled to forget everything about her death and even about her life.

He then went back to his therapist and made extremely rapid progress.

Fugue States

There is a small group of people whose potential for hypnosis is so high that, on a scale from 0 to 4, they would score 5. Given certain circumstances, they are candidates for the extreme symptoms of the "grade 5 syndrome," more commonly known as fugue states. These symptoms include multiple personality, extended regression to childhood, and *total* amnesia. Because so much of their consciousness is divorced from reality, people with these conditions tend to seem bizarre. However, these massively disruptive symptoms do not necessarily indicate severe psychopathology. Instead, they are an indication of a capacity gone wild. Although the unusually high potential for spontaneous trance can be most helpful in dealing with stress, when this potential goes awry, as can occasionally happen, the resulting problems are correspondingly extreme.

For instance, one ordinary reaction to stress is to flee from it psychologically. While it is common for people to try to distance themselves from a painful reality by mentally standing back or partially dissociating themselves from it, they do not usually leave behind their entire world. In rare instances, however, an individual escapes completely from an unbearable reality. Through an unintentional use of trance capacity, he or she imagines a better world and flees to it. This is what is called a "fugue" or flight state. People who enter a fugue state use dissociation to an extreme degree. It is as though a second reality were created in the imagination, consciousness was split, and the person entered a fantasy world. The trouble with this attempted solution to pain is that, in one way, it works too well. The person finds that it is not very difficult to escape from pain by running to the imagined other world and does so with increasing ease. The original problem is not solved but simply avoided, at the same time that more problems are added.

When a person has such a major dissociative event as entering a fugue state, hypnosis (or sodium pentathol) is useful in breaking through that massive symptom. As is the case with complex phobias, an additional part of hypnotic treatment consists of teaching the person to use trance on purpose rather than unconsciously sliding into it. Psychotherapy is indicated to resolve underlying conflicts.

A Case of Fugue

A nameless woman was admitted to an inpatient psychiatric unit because she was found wandering around as if in a fog. On the unit she responded minimally to questions by the staff. She was assigned to Dr. Marks for ongoing psychotherapy. Additionally, it was decided to try hypnosis to see if any light could be shed on her problem. Dr. Tracey, the hypnotist, found it difficult to get the patient's attention focused enough for trance. When finally hypnotized, however, she seemed to become alive. In trance, she reported no knowledge of being in the hospital. When asked, then, where she was, she replied that she was on a camping trip in the Canadian woods. She gave a vivid and detailed account of her experiences in the wild.

Dr. Tracey then helped her to try to become aware of her other experiences during the last few days. With prompting, she was able to say that she had a dreamlike memory of a person who looked like her wandering in the hospital. The ephemeral quality made it seem as though it were some kind of background nightmare to her camping trip.

In later hypnotic sessions, she remembered that the beginning of this episode had occurred when she saw her boyfriend meet another woman. This sight had upset her horribly for an instant. In the next moment, however, she found herself on the Canadian camping trip that he and she had often talked of making.

Having established the reason for her distress, she was able to begin to talk usefully about it in psychotherapy with Dr. Marks. Meanwhile, Dr. Tracey taught her how to control trance, and devoted one last session to some important hypnotic suggestions:

When you saw your boyfriend with another woman, you were afraid you would lose him, and that was very pain-

ful. Now, everyone likes to be relieved of pain. People say, "What you don't know won't hurt you." It's as though you have believed that old saying so strongly that you have convinced yourself not to recognize that you know some painful things by forgetting them. However, the cure is really worse than the disease. It is worse to have your life so horribly disrupted just to avoid knowing something, especially because even if you didn't know it, it would still be true. It is better to deal with a painful reality, with the help of your therapist, than to flee to a fantasy world. You agree with this, and you are not going to let this flight occur again. Now that you know how to use trance, you can tell the part of you that thinks it can avoid discomfort by forgetting, that you will not allow it. You will use your capacity for trance to restore memories rather than to erase them.

This patient had quickly been able to understand and control her use of trance capacity. She realized that the release from pain provided by her former use of trance was not worth the price of disruption of her life. She was discharged from the hospital and continued in psychotherapy to work on her sense of vulnerability to loss.

Multiple Personality

Cases of multiple personality have been made famous by such movies as *Sybil* and *The Three Faces of Eve*. Almost everyone is aware of different aspects of his own personality. Phrases such as "The devil made me do it" or "something inside of me" reflect a natural awareness of facets of the self. Some of these facets are, in varying degrees, unacceptable to the person. For someone with multiple personality, the part of the self that has these unacceptable feelings is walled off and made into a separate entity. Often, "personalities" differ in their awareness of each other. Some know of other personalities but are not in turn known. Frequently there is a master personality that is aware of all of them.

A Case of Multiple Personality

Harold Rogers, a forty-year-old married man, was brought to the attention of a psychiatric service by the emergency-room staff of a general hospital. His family insisted he see a doctor because he had been disappearing for days at a time and professed no knowledge of his whereabouts during these blackouts. Mr. Rogers was a member of a very strict fundamentalist religion. His sect permitted no drinking or dancing, and even playing Monopoly was considered a sin because the game used "the devil's bones" – dice.

The psychiatrist on call, Dr. Graves, recognized the fugue-state nature of these interludes and suggested hypnosis. In trance, Mr. Rogers was asked to let his consciousness go to sleep. He was then told that if there was anyone else present, this other somebody could now show himself. Mr. Rogers suddenly opened his eyes. His face was creased by a big grin, and in a booming voice, quite unlike his former sober, restrained manner of speech, he introduced himself as George Harley. Slapping hands with the "Doc," he suggested adjourning to a local pub.

As his story unfolded, George explained that Harold never wanted to have any fun. Harold was the devout son of a preacher, and Harold's father would have been awfully upset at George's idea of fun. George related that he was the spirit of a boyhood friend with whom Harold used to sneak out and "do things." Nowadays, George spent his days watching Harold lead his pious, restricted life until he could stand it no longer. Then he would wrestle with Harold, knock him out, and go to a nearby town where he was quite well known in certain quarters. After several riotous days and nights, he would collapse, his money and energy spent, and Harold would resume control of their body. Harold would feel as though he had slept for the last few days.

As in most such cases, simply identifying the crude dramatization of conflict between impulses and forces to contain them did not solve the problem. It was clear that Harold had to come to grips with his whole personality, including the "sinful" elements of it.

Harold needed long-term help, and he was referred to a psychologist for psychotherapy. Whenever his therapist felt hypnosis could be useful, Harold would return to Dr. Graves for a session. One such time came while Harold was trying to learn to understand and reconcile different aspects of personality.

In trance he was told,

> *In the past, you have learned how to bring out first one,*
> *then a second "personality," practicing returning first*

one, then the other. You see how with hypnosis you have been able to bring both of your personalities out in these sessions. In this way we can see that both of these personalities are part of you. You are a man who has different aspects of himself. For most people, having different aspects of themselves is taken for granted. A person can be both a family man and a worker, a child of his parents and a father to his children, a sexual being and a pious churchgoer, et cetera. For you, some of your different aspects, feelings, urges, or wishes seemed so difficult to reconcile that it was as though they were different people. However, when you've tried to reconcile your urges by having different people in you, you found that didn't work. When George went on a bender, Harold was absent from the family just as if he had gone on the bender. When George drinks, Harold's body holds the alcohol in it. If George develops an illness or is injured, Harold also pays the price.

Wherever George is, Harold is also. By separating George and Harold, you've made it impossible for Harold to work his restraining influence on George. Conversely, by burying George so deeply most of the time, when the impulses erupt they are so overwhelming as to be nearly uncontrolled.

You see that George and Harold are both parts of the same individual who is you. In therapy you are going to have to learn ways for disparate feelings to live together. You are going to have to learn how to make both George and Harold content and satisfied. If George and Harold were to keep splitting off and being unaware of each other, it would make it all the more difficult to work

*out an accommodation between them. Because of that,
both you and your therapist needed to know how to bring
back one personality when he is lost. Now, if one tries to
take over, the other, aided by your therapist, will use your
ability to go into trance, not to separate the "personalities" further, as you did in the past, but rather to bring
them together, healing rather than dividing.*

*Each of the aspects of personality has advantages for
certain situations. Sometimes you are going to want a lot
more of Harold in the forefront. Sometimes George's special abilities will be particularly useful. At these times
you will do what other people do – let the most useful aspect of your individual personality come to the fore. That
part of yourself will be strongest, or most evident, but
you will always be ultimately in control.*

The first step in Harold's treatment was identifying
the use of fugue. Next, it was necessary for him to stop
using this outlet for his urges. The final task was long-
term resolution of his conflicts. Hypnosis was vital for
the first step and useful in the second as a way of teaching
Harold to control his natural capacity for trance. The
third task was the province of traditional psychotherapy,
hypnosis being used to strengthen constructive learning.

Conversion Reactions

Conversion reactions may be less totally upsetting than
fugue but are similar in genesis. In contrast to the splitting of the entire personality, a part of the body is chosen
as the site of conflict.

Successful treatment of a person with a conversion reaction must take into account the pride of the victim. To say to someone with paralyzed legs, "Arise and walk," may work in the context of an evangelical prayer meeting. When divine intervention is credited with change, it is expected to work dramatically. However, if a *doctor* were to say, "Get up and walk," or, "There's nothing wrong with your legs, so stop having that symptom," and the symptom did disappear, the patient would look like a malingerer. The conscious mind requires an explanation for the removal of a symptom of unconscious conflict.

Hypnosis can provide a useful, though limited, tool in the gradual recovery of the affected limbs. When full function becomes possible in trance, as occasionally happens, it can sometimes be slowly transferred to the waking state. Otherwise, a feeling of life gradually returning to a numb limb can be suggested. Nevertheless, any final cure rests on a resolution of the underlying conflict.

A Case of Conversion Reaction

A young woman, Ellen Kendrick, left her family's rural Kansas farmhouse and moved to New York City. She was fearful, at one level, that she might give vent to her "wild" impulses if she went out at night. She was unwilling, however, to go back to the "safety" of the farm. She developed paralysis in her legs, which kept her from going either place.

The hypnotic treatment of Ellen's paralyzed legs consisted of suggestions that evolved *gradually* (over the course of four sessions) into full recovery of their use.

147

This suggested recovery would no doubt have failed if she had not also been discussing her conflicts with a psychiatrist.

During the series of hypnotic sessions, Ellen was told,

> [Session 1] *I'd like you to feel and become aware of a sensation in your fingertips, perhaps a tingling sensation. As it becomes strong, you bring your fingers down to your lower limbs and transfer the sensation to the legs. It may continue as a tingling sensation, or it may be somewhat different. It will be interesting to find out how it feels. As the feeling gets stronger, you can remove your hand and let that feeling continue to be strong through your legs. It feels as though they are coming back to life slowly but steadily. You can feel individual muscle cells contract as life returns to them. Your legs are not strong enough to walk on, but you are feeling the nerves reconnecting the motor area of your brain to your legs.*
>
> [Session 2] *That's right. As those sensations and sense of control have grown stronger in your legs, you feel able to begin to press down on the floor. Feel the sensation of your legs pressing down on the floor. In fact, it's impossible to prevent your legs from pressing down on the floor. And now, while one leg continues to press down, I'd like you to imagine the other leg becoming very light and lifting itself off the floor. Let it lift, then return.*
>
> [Session 3] *As your legs are stronger, able to press on floor and to lift in the air, you realize you have been doing, in a controlled way, what your legs do when you stand and walk. Let's see if you can do that. Of course,*

your legs are weak and may need support to help them build up their strength, but you know that you have re-learned the connection between your brain and legs. Now you need practice.

[Session 4] Now that you have been walking, you realize something of how your mind and body interacted. As you've been discussing with your therapist, you have had a conflict that showed up in your legs. When people told you, "It's all in your head" and "Nothing is wrong," they were wrong, because you could not consciously make your legs work. A part of your brain which at that time was outside of your control was giving your legs the orders not to work. Now, however, you have learned to control that part as well, so you need never fear future symptoms like this. Should they try to erupt, you know how to handle them.

"Getting Stuck" in Hypnosis

The idea of finding oneself unable to leave trance strikes a fearful chord in many people. For the most part, this frightening idea has more to do with fantasy than with actual reality. A patient may occasionally reach the end of a therapy session that has involved hypnosis and then declare that he is still in a trance. "Because I cannot stop being hypnotized," he or she might declare, "I had better not leave." This stall is, in essence, the same as the case of a nonhypnotized patient who says at the end of a session, "I can't leave because I have things I still have to talk about." A competent therapist would handle both patients in the same manner.

There are cases of stage hypnosis, however, when the trance continues well past the conclusion of the scheduled entertainment. Such instances tend to cause a stir when the stage hypnotist doesn't know how to handle the "unending" trance.

A Case of Unconscious Revenge

Constance Hughes was a seventeen-year-old woman who was raised in strict accordance with the prevailing fundamentalist religion of her Bible Belt community. On a visit to her cousin's town, however, Constance was persuaded to attend a performance of "Professor Marvello's Marvelous Mesmerism."

Once seated in the audience, Constance was urged by her giggling cousin to volunteer in one of the hypnotist's acts. Eventually she allowed herself to be coaxed onto the stage by Marvello. Being very hypnotizable, Constance entered trance and, like a person with multiple personality, let her dissociated self go along with the hypnotist's risqué suggestions. Normally, she would have been shocked at her own actions. However, Constance could seize this opportunity to "misbehave" because she did not have to assume any responsibility for her own fantasies. Simultaneously, at another level, Constance was aware of her own guilt and was furious with the hypnotist for seducing her into improper behavior.

At the conclusion of the act, her guilt and anger combined to make Constance unconsciously unwilling to give up trance. By not coming out of it, she strengthened her self-perception that she was "made to do those bad things" and could not control herself. Further, she got the satisfaction of seeing the hypnotist scared and humiliated by his inability to "bring her back."

As revenge, it worked marvelously. The Professor became panic-stricken. It was clear to everyone that Marvello had *made* Constance do things, and he had lost control of the situation. Furthermore, Constance unconsciously enjoyed the swarm of attentive people around her. When a photographer from the local newspaper took a picture of her lying helpless on the stage, a part of her rejoiced in achieving celebrity. Finally, she was loaded into an ambulance and rushed to the hospital.

Fortunately, there was a competent psychologist on call who knew how to handle psychological distress without exploiting it. Dr. Bond proceeded to take the entranced Constance through another, nonthreatening hypnotic induction, briefly explored with her why she felt unable to leave trance, acknowledged with her what strong feelings she had toward the stage hypnotist, and then helped her to grant herself forgiveness for what she did on stage. Telling her it was safe to leave trance, he then gave her two suggestions:

> *As soon as you are feeling safe, you will be able to count backward from ten. At one, you will be fully alert and your usual sensations and control will have returned. If you don't feel safe soon, though, you will find that you will fall asleep. When you awaken, you will wake up in the usual state of alertness. Sleep is a natural antidote to hypnosis.*

8
Habit Control

The most popularly known and best advertised use of hypnosis is for habit control. A look through the Yellow Pages will probably show ads for hypnosis to stop smoking or lose weight. Hypnosis is also used to treat a great variety of other habits: nail biting, hair pulling, enuresis, alcohol and drug abuse, teeth grinding, and any other behavior that has assumed an independent and unwanted existence as a habit.

The theoretical basis for such treatment is not as strong as it is for the use of trance with either dissociative disorders, such as phobias and hysterical symptoms, or the control of pain. The capacity for trance is not essential to the development of a habit, nor is the distortion of perception, so helpful in pain relief, a necessary part of changing a habit.

Nonetheless, hypnosis can be useful in unlearning and modifying patterns for a number of reasons. First, the use of hypnosis per se tends to raise both the patient's and the therapist's expectations of success. Next, people often use habitual behavior as a means of tension release. Hypnosis can reduce tension and so serves to lessen the need for the habit. Third, because hypnosis is a method of imagining behavior or action, it can allow a person to "practice" new, desirable behaviors and replace old, habitual ones. Coupling this "practice" with relaxation or any of a variety of other responses conditions the individual to different behavior. Fourth, hypnotic distortion of sensation, while not necessary, can be helpful in modifying habits (e.g., making it more painful to bite fingernails). Finally, hypnosis may be most useful in developing an imagery that strengthens an individual's reasons for wanting change.

This list is not meant to suggest that we always know why hypnosis works. Sometimes it is successful for no known reason, even when no other treatment has touched the habit. In general, the more a habit is just a familiar way of behaving that has no current value, conscious or unconscious, the easier it is to break. As the following cases will show, the most important factor in habit change is *motivation*.

Smoking

People who wish to stop smoking often arrive for hypnosis with a variety of motivations, different degrees of resolve, and mixed feelings or desires. For instance, one patient wrote:

Dear Dr. Myer,

After leaving your office yesterday I felt, for the first time, that I had the power never to have another cigarette. At first, the thought was pleasant and exciting. As

I continued to think about it, though, I thought, "What would it be like to be at a cocktail party without smoking?" I decided it would be terrible. In fact, I realized I do not wish to stop smoking. I used to say, "I want to stop but cannot." Now I realize I can stop but do not want to do so.

In a similar vein, one married woman was the only smoker in her athletic, health-oriented family. Under a barrage of requests, demands, and complaints, she agreed to be "hypnotized out of smoking." However, she had no personal desire to stop. Instead, her plan seemed to be to say to her family, "Look, I tried. I even went to a hypnotist. I guess I just cannot quit. (So stop pestering me.)" Under such circumstances, hypnosis was bound to fail and hence was not even attempted. Instead, this woman was told that if at any future date *she*, not her family, wanted to learn to control her urge to smoke, she was welcome to return.

When motivation is internal and the individual's own desire to stop is genuine (even though not without regrets), breaking the smoking habit is relatively simple: one needs only never to light up again. Since total abstinence tends to be easier than continual moderation, nonsmoking is much less complicated than, for instance, losing weight. One can simply never smoke again, but one cannot simply never eat again. Additionally, nonsmoking avoids another problem inherent in habits such as hair pulling or fingernail biting. One can consciously choose to stay away from tobacco stores or put physical distance between himself and temptation. One cannot, however, so easily remove oneself from one's hair or fingernails.

Although it is clear that many people find nonsmoking extremely difficult, the degree of difficulty is often exaggerated. Many of those who have quit enjoy fostering the idea that quitting is pretty impossible, for it shows what heroic, iron-willed individuals they are. The common boast or complaint, "I stopped smoking twenty years ago, and I still miss it," has less substance than posturing ("My willpower has lasted twenty years"). Those who have tried to quit and failed are even more motivated to paint the task as herculean. ("Of course I couldn't stop. No one can.") Confronted with an "unbreakable habit," some smokers turn to hypnosis as though to some kind of magic.

Some of the more flamboyant hypnotic approaches overlook the role of motivation and control in a way that renders treatment useless. For instance, the coach of a professional basketball team once went to a hypnotist to stop smoking. He was apparently quite a good subject, and a cure for smoking was attempted. First, before hypnosis, a drop of iodine was placed on his tongue, which he found most distasteful. Next, hypnosis was induced. In hypnosis, it was suggested that cigarettes tasted like iodine, and that to puff on a cigarette would produce a very vivid taste of iodine on the tongue. The hallucinated taste was apparently as vivid as described, for when told to light a cigarette, the coach did so. He then quickly disposed of it, complaining of the bad taste. It was suggested that this effect would continue when he was out of hypnosis. The trance was then ended.

Out of hypnosis, the coach was offered a cigarette. He lit it, then put it out in disgust, saying it tasted like iodine. He was then told cigarettes would taste so bad that he would never smoke again. The grateful coach thanked the hypnotist and left.

Several months later, a local sportswriter, who knew this story, entered the basketball players' locker room following the team's tough loss. There he found the coach smoking.

"What happened? Did the suggestion wear off?" asked the writer.

"No," said the coach. "They taste awful. They taste like iodine, but I still want to smoke."

Hypnosis can be helpful, however, in altering or influencing the urge to smoke. That is, the best hypnotic strategy is to make the *urge* to smoke the target, leaving the *action* of smoking up to the patient.

A Case of Heavy Smoking

Mr. Levy, a personable, successful man, requested hypnosis to stop smoking. In taking a history, Dr. Brines found he had begun to smoke as a freshman in college. He had tried to quit three or four times, to no avail. During one of these times, Mr. Levy had managed to abstain for six months. At that point, he had gone to a party, where he drank too much and borrowed a cigarette. The next day he felt that he had broken his resolve and returned to smoking at his previous level of two packs a day.

When Dr. Brines asked Mr. Levy why he wanted to quit smoking, he expressed surprise that she did not just assume anyone would want to – that was what one was supposed to do. She told him that it was *his* motivation that had kept him smoking and that only his motivation, not the Surgeon General's, was pertinent. Mr. Levy then stated that he wanted to quit because he had concerns about the long-term effects on his health and an aware-ness of the effect of smoking on his stamina. During his routine jogging, he found himself very quickly out of breath. Additionally, no one in his social circle smoked, and he felt uncomfortably conspicuous with these friends. Finally, since he was unable to control an urge, Mr. Levy felt as if he were demonstrating a weakness in his character whenever he lit up.

Because of Mr. Levy's strong motivation, treatment for this habit seemed likely to succeed. Therefore, follow-ing the hypnotic induction and the usual remarks about the increasing ease of reinductions, Dr. Brines and Mr. Levy went to work on smoking. The doctor told Mr. Levy about strategies for stopping. People who smoke in all sorts of situations, for whom every mood, situation, location, and time of day is a cue for a cigarette, have the most success and the least distress if they quit "cold turkey" rather than cut down. They are like alcoholics. They cannot smoke, just as the alcoholic cannot drink, in anything approaching moderation. Dr. Brines contin-ued by pointing out that saying to oneself, "I don't want a cigarette" is a poor strategy because it is so patently false. Such a statement also calls to mind the image of a cigarette and thus increases desire. Positive suggestions

158

almost always work better than negative ones, Dr. Brines informed him. He needed something to do, not something not to do.

She then gave Mr. Levy a series of three ideas or thoughts he could use to control his urge to smoke. The first was "Smoking is a poison to your body." Mr. Levy enjoyed smoking and found it a pleasure, a source of relaxation, and something to do with his hands. For his body, however, it was dangerous. He knew that cigarettes were implicated in cancer, emphysema, and circulatory problems. The ill effects were becoming apparent in his decreased stamina and lack of "wind." He could hear his smoker's cough. If he thought back to the very first time he ever smoked, he would remember feeling sick or slightly "green." That was his body's way of saying it was being poisoned. Dr. Brines stated the first idea once more, saying, "Smoking is a poison to your body."

The next idea presented was, "You need your body to live." Dr. Brines told Mr. Levy that when his body died, he died. While he was alive, furthermore, the quality and style of his life were limited by his body's limits. "If," she said, "you want to run a marathon, but your lungs wheeze at even a brisk walk, your life will not include marathons. If your social circle consists of non-smokers, your body's smoking produces a barrier or problem in these relationships." Once again, she stated the second idea – "You need your body to live."

Dr. Brines then presented a third idea to Mr. Levy: "You owe it to yourself to care for your body. One way you care for it is by not smoking." The doctor continued by telling him that he knew smoking hurt his body even though he enjoyed it. He was then in a position to make a choice. He could either have a cigarette and hurt his body, which he needed to live, or he could give up the pleasure of smoking while gaining the pleasure of a healthier, longer life span.

At this point, Dr. Brines said,

You make many such choices in life. You bring your car in for a tune-up not because it is fun to do so. In fact, it can be a real nuisance. You bring it in because you must do so if you want a dependable means of transportation. Sometimes, when you wake up on Monday morning, it would be pleasant to roll over and go back to sleep, yet you get up. It is not that it wouldn't be nice to remain in bed, but rather that you are choosing the pleasures and satisfactions of being responsible, earning money, and being productive at work.

As you are choosing to take good care of your body, you will not hurt it by substituting the health hazard of overeating for that of smoking. You will not exchange cigarettes for food.

Dr. Brines suggested that Mr. Levy would be reminded of these three ideas and would feel relaxed whenever he touched his cheek. He was instructed to practice hypnosis at least three times a day. If he found it inconvenient to hypnotize himself, he was to touch his cheek, feel himself relax, and think of the three ideas. If he found himself reaching for a cigarette, he was not to stop the movement, but rather to change it to touching his cheek.

She suggested, "Just as a judo expert uses the force of his opponent's blow by redirecting it, so you will turn the urge to smoke into a reminder of your wish to care for yourself."

They arranged an appointment for the following week, and Mr. Levy was told to call during the next seven days if he needed to.

When Mr. Levy returned for his second session, he reported that he had been able to practice his hypnotic exercise regularly and had controlled his urge to smoke. He felt that doing so required much effort, however. He wanted more help. Doctor and patient briefly discussed the role of his motivation and struggle in continuing not to smoke, then moved on to hypnosis.

In trance, the following suggestions were made.

Imagine a bucket of hot tar boiling in this office. Think of how that tar would burn and stain if you were to touch it. Tar and feathers were once used as a punishment for that very reason. Think of how the chemicals would stain and seep into your skin. Now imagine a white straw sitting in the bucket of tar. Think how terrible it would be to suck even a tiny bit into your mouth, how it would burn and hurt the delicate tissues. No one could pay you to do it. And how much worse it is to contemplate swallowing that drop of tar!

Even swallowing it is not the worst, because the tar could pass through your body and be eliminated. Imagine sucking it into your lungs. Think of how it would coat or clog the delicate passages. How it would choke you. How oxygen could not pass through the membranes of your lungs to get to your blood.

You realize that the straw is a cigarette, and every time you smoke, the fire at the tip melts the tar, and you draw it into your lungs. It has happened in small enough doses to let you ignore it and kid yourself that it did not matter. Now it has added up. Your lungs are coated with tar. You feel sad because you realize how you have been hurting yourself.

Now you realize you need not feel so bad. You have stopped smoking. Your lungs can start to fight back, to cleanse themselves. In just six months, they'll be able to become as clean and pink as new. You are very glad it is not too late.

Now, let's change to another scene. The bucket of tar is gone. You are relaxed and at peace. Imagine that there on the table before you is a pack of your favorite brand of cigarettes. Reach over and pick it up. Feel the familiar weight, shape, and texture. Now open the pack. Smell the fresh tobacco. Take one out, roll it in your fingers, tamp down the tobacco. Now draw it across your nostrils. Realize that it would taste good, that a part of you wants to smoke.

Now touch your cheek, relax, and think of your three ideas. Smoking is a poison to your body. You need your body to live. You owe it to yourself to care for your body. One way you do so is by not smoking. You realize that even when most tantalized by cigarettes, you still retain the ability to relax and remember why you choose to take care of yourself and, once again, that one way you care for yourself is by not smoking.

162

Dr. Brines had Mr. Levy end trance. He was urged to continue his exercises and call from time to time just to check in. If he had any trouble, he was to come back for another appointment.

Two years later, a new patient came in requesting hypnosis to stop smoking. He had been referred by his friend Mr. Levy, who was still not smoking.

Other Suggestions for Stopping Smoking

There are countless other types of hypnotic suggestions that can be used for breaking the smoking habit, depending on the personality and needs of the patient. The list that follows by no means exhausts the possibilities.

DEATH OF A CIGARETTE. A therapist might notice that for one patient, cigarettes seem like a friend. To that patient he might say, "Imagine a funeral scene. There in the coffin is a carton of your favorite cigarettes. As is typical of a funeral of a loved one, you are saddened by the prospect of life without your friend. Such grief is expectable and legitimate. However, sad as you may be, you will not jump into the grave to stay with the dead. Cigarettes are dead, but you are alive and committed to life."

THE HAPPY NONSMOKER. The hypnotist could instruct, "Recall a pleasant time when you were not smoking; then go back to that time to relive vividly that experience. Perhaps such a time was while you were walking in the woods, while swimming, at a movie, or in church. For that time you were a nonsmoker. Feel how it is to be a nonsmoker. Realize that this time could easily be stretched by a few minutes, an hour, a day, a week. See how the sensation can grow and continue, how nonsmoking is a familiar, if brief, past experience."

THE BALL AND CHAIN. "Imagine a convict's ball and chain attached to your ankle. Substitute a pack of cigarettes for the ball. Feel how you have always been lugging smokes around, how you feel enslaved by them. Recall times scrounging through the ashtray for long butts, or going to the store at 2:00 A.M. for cigarettes. Break the chain and realize how free it feels to be no longer manacled to cigarettes."

CANCER. "Imagine being in the doctor's office. The doctor comes in looking grim. He sadly shakes his head and says, 'It's cancer. We'll have to remove your larynx. You'll never speak again.' Feel the horror, the wish to have stopped smoking while there was still time. Then realize it is not too late."

TELEPHONE JOY. "Imagine being on the telephone, comfortable and relaxed, and not smoking. Picture yourself drinking coffee without a cigarette. Imagine being happy and relaxed and not smoking in all the situations you formerly associated with cigarettes."

OVERSMOKING. "Force yourself to smoke without a break, cigarette after cigarette, like a goose being force-fed for pâté. When you cannot take another puff, stop. Next, while hypnotized, vividly recall the disgusted feeling of oversmoking and your decision to stop. Repeat the hypnotic recall saying, 'This is what smoking really is.'"

THE GIFT. "Imagine how not smoking is a present of health to yourself."

Group Approach

People frequently join groups to try to stop smoking. Different groups use different behavioral approaches, one of which may be hypnosis. While hypnosis is a state that takes place within an individual, an individual need not be alone in order to be hypnotized. He or she may just as easily enter trance in the midst of a group. As is the case with the Harvard Group Scale, one induction can be given to a number of people en masse.

When people are gathered to stop smoking, the leader (hypnotist) starts off a typical first session by pointing out that individual differences in response exist and that it is not a sign that something is wrong if members do not do or feel exactly what the hypnotist describes. He then induces trance for the group. All of the suggestions and images mentioned for individual treatment can be adapted for group purposes. In fact, the leader might very well present the same three ideas used in Mr. Levy's treatment to the group.

Over the course of six to eight sessions, members spend part of each meeting in unhypnotized discussions about problems and progress. The remaining time is used for hypnotic suggestions. The group leader does not know if any specific issue is to the point for any specific member of the group, but he assumes that many people will respond to many of the suggestions. This assumption is borne out by the number of people who do manage to stop smoking with this method.

The main difference between individual and group hypnotic inductions is that, in the case of the latter, there must be less personalization of the material. For example, some people in a group respond to the suggestion of eye closure more quickly than others. Thus, when the hypnotist is addressing a group, some of its members will have eyes closed, while others will be wide-eyed and alert. The hypnotist must modify his statements so as to exclude no one. Since he cannot say, "Your eyes are closed," he might substitute, "Your eyelids feel heavy." Similarly, certain responses that are suitable in an individual session are disruptive in a group setting. A hypnotist might very well say to an individual patient, for instance, "Tell me to which place you have floated." Because talking out loud would distract other group members, the hypnotist might instead suggest that each member write the imagined location on a piece of paper. All feedback must be more vague and targeted to the general audience. Each person can then interpret the hypnotist's remarks according to his or her own experience.

Perhaps the most common problem for *any* task-oriented group, not just hypnotic or nonsmoking groups, has to do with group dynamics. In a well-run group, members usually want to be similar to each other. There is a strong tendency toward acceptance of group norms and standards of behavior. If a group is both overtly and covertly working to stop smoking, for example, all will be well. Sometimes, however, group pressure works against rather than for the stated goal. A "break the smoking habit" group can end up meeting to discuss how impossible it is to stop smoking. Instead of being a group to stop smoking, it becomes a support group for smokers who say they wish to quit but who agree it is impossible. The unfortunate individual who *really* wishes to stop and finds himself in such a group is forced to choose either to give up both the group support and cigarettes or continue to smoke until the group has concluded.

Overeating

Many people who suffer from excessive weight do not know what it is to feel "hungry." Studies have shown that overweight individuals are so out of touch with their bodies' sensations that they tend to eat only according to a variety of external cues, such as time of day or certain surroundings, rather than according to an internal sense of being hungry. For instance, if such a person were given a dull task and a false time frame (provided by a clock that runs very fast or very slow), he would eat lunch when the clock said noon, even if it were only 10:00 A.M. Conversely, the same person would not eat lunch at noon if the clock said 10:00 A.M. Without an internal sense of how much food is enough to satisfy hunger, it becomes easy to overeat and thus become overweight.

Proper treatment of excessive weight by means of hypnosis is always done in conjunction with some regimen that directly affects weight. That is, one does not simply hypnotize a heavy individual, command him to be skinny, then watch the pounds disappear in the twinkling of an eye. To lose weight he must eat less or burn up more calories.

Additionally, the common request to make food taste bad — "Make chocolate taste bad so I won't eat it," for instance — is useless in practice. The request could easily be accomplished with hypnosis. However, the individual subject to this taste distortion would soon find himself eating chocolate that tasted like mud rather than decreasing his chocolate intake. In much the same way do children continue to suck their thumbs despite the application of foul-tasting substances.

The hypnotic treatment of the overweight consists of a series of hypnotic exercises, the number and order of which may vary according to patients' needs and time constraints. Such exercises, whether taught to individuals or groups, are designed to promote and maintain good eating habits, to make identifiable and control the sensations associated with hunger, and to ease the adaptation from fat to thin. These hypnotic tasks, however, must *always* be accompanied by a physical weight-loss method, whether it be fasting, dieting, calorie counting, or exercising.

Weight Loss in a Group Setting

The nutrition and psychiatry departments of a general hospital joined together to offer a group program using hypnosis for weight loss. Groups were open to any reasonably healthy adult who had a problem of excess weight. Referrals were made by the staff of the hospital. Self-referrals were also accepted.

The program offered one meeting per week for ten consecutive weeks. Groups were designed to be no smaller than eight and no larger than fifteen members. Each group offered a combination of nutritional counseling, group support for the task of losing weight, and hypnotic strategies to help in this task.

The co-leaders of one of these groups were Mary Lyons, a nutritionist, and Dr. Joan Smith, a psychiatric resident trained in hypnosis. The leaders worked as a team, each assuming more responsibility for the area of her expertise. Ms. Lyons was in charge of nutritional counseling, planning diets, and monitoring weight change. Dr. Smith was responsible for all hypnotic aspects of the treatment. Both leaders had had experience in group dynamics, Dr. Smith from the practice of group psychotherapy and Ms. Lyons from running previous weight-loss groups. Thus they shared responsibility for helping individuals function as a supportive, task-oriented group.

One of their typical groups consisted of nine women and three men who ranged from ten to seventy pounds above ideal weight (by their own estimates.) Each person in the group had tried a variety of weight-loss methods in the past, none with much success. Most were in generally good health, but one suffered from diabetes, two from hypertension. These three had been referred by their internists, who continued to monitor their health and oversee their diets.

When they came to the first meeting, all of the group members were a little apprehensive. Most of the nervousness had to do with the prospect of using hypnosis.

Thus, Dr. Smith devoted the first part of the session to helping members air wishes and fears regarding trance, and to correcting their misperceptions. Next, Ms. Lyons took over to discuss the diet plan that she was recommending. She favored an approach based on reduced caloric intake within the framework of a balanced diet. When the nutritional guidelines had been set, Dr. Smith once again led the group. She gave them a Head Falling Forward suggestion with no trance involved. The doctor wanted the group to have the experience of responding to a suggestion outside of hypnosis since she felt that doing so might alleviate some of their nervousness about trance. As anxiety decreased, she expected the group members would be increasingly able to participate in hypnosis.

Dr. Smith next went through a group hypnotic induction. No specific suggestions regarding food were made at this time, but members were told how to reenter the state so that they might use self-hypnosis in the future. Following this exercise, the group discussed the hypnotic experience as well as their expectations for upcoming sessions. They left this first session with instructions to practice hypnosis daily and with information about their diets for the week.

Over the course of the next nine weeks, the group continued meeting. At each meeting, much of the time was devoted to discussion and nutritional issues. The remaining time was used by Dr. Smith to teach new hypnotic exercises. A session-by-session account of each exercise (in condensed form) follows.

Session 2: Four Ideas

Relax, picture a nice, peaceful scene, and feel very calm. Touch your cheek, and make an association between the sensation of touching your cheek and a sense of relaxation. Next, think of four ideas while relaxed:

1. Food is fuel for your body. *Food is not a reward if you are good, solace if you are sad, or a friend if you are lonely.*

2. Too much fuel hurts your body. *Too much food turns into fat. It puts a strain on your heart, lungs, and muscles.*

3. You need your body to live. *When your body dies, you die. Being overweight shortens your life. While you are alive, the kind and style of life are limited by your body.*

4. If you take good care of your body, it will reward you by feeling and looking good. *You eat well because it is in your own best interest.*

Think of the relationship among these ideas. This association will maintain itself even when you are not hypnotized. Also, when you touch your cheek, you will remember to relax and think of these ideas. Relaxing leads to a lessening of tension, which leads to less need to eat out of anxiety.

Session 3: "Dine," Not "Feed"

Imagine a very nice meal set out before you. See the table, dining companions, and table settings. See the good food. Look at it. Smell it. Now put a small, perfect serving on your plate. Observe and appreciate it.

Now choose the best-looking bite. Remember that the first bite will taste the best because your taste buds are fresh. Cut a small portion. Put it in your mouth, and set your knife and fork down. Concentrate on the taste of the food. Notice its texture. Notice how the flavor is a subtle blend of various elements. Take time, and when all the pleasure has been extracted, swallow.

Notice that you put down your knife and fork. This is not an assembly line. Enjoy dining. Take time to enjoy the food, and don't have your whole meal precut, ready for shoveling in and quickly swallowing. Remember, it takes about twenty minutes for your brain to register the food and make you feel full.

Now have a drink of water. Then decide to have a sip of whatever else you are drinking with your meal – wine, juice, or whatever. Look at the color of it. Smell it. Then take a small sip of it. Roll it around on your tongue. Notice the taste. Swallow. Remember, water is to quench thirst; wine or other drinks are to sip for taste.

Proceed through your entire meal like this, taking small portions, savoring the food, putting down your knife and fork between bites, having drinks of water and small sips of your drink.

172

Throughout, stress the pleasure of tasting *small quantities rather than shoveling down larger volume and ignoring taste. Compare the difference between a fine gourmet restaurant with its small, perfect nouvelle cuisine servings and an old, all-you-can-eat-for-$2.49 joint. Begin to feel full. Stop eating.*

Session 4: Shrinking Stomach

Hold out your arm and make a muscle. Feel how strong and powerful it is. Feel the strong, good power of the muscle. Relax. Now do it again, but this time feel your arm becoming cramped and painful. Feel the cramp in your arm becoming worse and worse. Relax.

See how both actions were physically identical. The same message of muscle tightness was sent to your brain, but your brain interpreted the first time as a good feeling, the second as painful. In the same way, hunger can be a matter of how you interpret a signal.

The experience of hunger occurs, in part, in the stomach. This sensation happens when your stomach muscles contract farther and farther without hitting anything. Your stomach is empty. If you fill your stomach with something, even an inflated balloon, it feels "full." So here's a suggestion.

Feel your stomach muscles tighten and contract. As they do, feel what a good feeling it is. Your stomach is shrinking. This is a good sign, for soon your whole body will begin to grow thinner. That's right. Your stomach is getting smaller and smaller. Soon your body will get smaller and smaller too. This does not signal anything bad. You are not in danger. You are not dying of hunger. This is a good feeling of health, of a shrinking stomach. You would hate to lose this feeling by eating too much and stretching your stomach out. This feeling is not a hunger pain, *it is a powerful sense of shrinking, just as your whole body will soon shrink and become more slender.*

Session 5: See Yourself Thin

Picture yourself in a large room with a full-length mirror, perhaps like a ballet studio. Look around. Look at yourself in the mirror. As you watch yourself, imagine yourself becoming thinner and thinner, more and more trim. Your body remains its current age, your hair length and color are the same, but your body is trimmer and firmer, closer and closer to your ideal weight. Look at yourself. You are dressed so that you can see your body. See how you look. Feel how you feel. Feel your body move, how easily you can exercise and move about. Your limbs are light and strong. Your breathing is easier; your heart is less strained.

Often, as people lose weight, they look in the mirror and see a stranger. They feel ill at ease in this new shape. As you practice this exercise, you will come to see that this thin person is you. You will feel, as you lose weight, that you are looking more and more like "yourself."

174

Session 6: Regular Mealtime

Picture yourself at the dinner table. Eat until you feel bloated and stuffed. Feel sick from overeating. Now you are sorry. Then, imagine yourself eating slowly from small portions. After dinner you feel healthy and satisfied. Which would you rather feel one hour after your meal – sick or healthy?

Session 6: Buffet

Picture yourself at a buffet table. Go down one side and mound huge portions of everything on your plate. See yourself in a carnival mirror, becoming rounder and rounder. Go down the other side of the table, taking small, select portions. See yourself in the mirror as more and more slim and healthy.

Session 7: Holiday Meal

Imagine yourself at a holiday meal where everyone is urging you to eat more and you feel under a lot of pressure to do so. How do you say no? Rehearse your answers. Remember, you are eating for you, *not for relatives or friends. Take small, select portions of food.*

Session 7: Reward

When you eat small amounts you are taking good care of yourself. This is a present to yourself, not a sense of deprivation or something bad for you.

Session 8: Garbage Can

When there is more food on a plate than you need, the leftover scraps go into the garbage can. If you eat more than you need, you are treating yourself like a garbage can.

Session 8: Bankbook

Picture a bankbook with your allotted amount of calories as the balance. Each time you eat, deduct the proper amount from the balance.

Session 9: Lean and Athletic

Picture yourself walking in spring. A thinner you walks more quickly in summer. Come fall, as you become still more slender, see yourself jogging. In winter, a fit and trim you goes skating, skis, or plays in the snow.

Session 10: Review Previously Learned Exercises

As is true for participants in any weight-loss program, the group members who were most motivated to lose weight did so. Weight loss was not correlated with degree of hypnotizability but rather with the extent to which each person worked at and stuck to his or her diet. One person dropped out after two sessions, disappointed that there was not some magic to make pounds disappear. The remaining members lost from three to twenty-five pounds. Most of the people felt that hypnosis enabled them to channel their motivation more effectively than any other method they had previously tried.

Marijuana and Alcohol

There are a substantial number of people who cannot use alcohol or drugs in a controlled way. The effects of un-controlled use are severe, having individual, familial, and social ramifications. Because of the complex intrapsychic and interpersonal factors that lead to alcohol or drug abuse, treatment must take into account all contributing forces. Alcoholics Anonymous, for example, has been most successful in the treatment of alcohol abuse. Its approach combines group dynamics, practical interven-tions with individual support, and recognition of physi-ological effects. Anything short of this is not likely to help the alcoholic.

On the other hand, many people are able to enjoy the mild intoxication that come from a *moderate* use of marijuana or alcohol and wish to keep their use to this level. When physical addiction is not a problem, and the goal is not total abstinence, hypnosis can help. Changing habitual, moderate drug or alcohol use is rather like los-ing five to ten unnecessary pounds. Just as hypnosis can help with a change in eating habits, so it can help in the slight modification of nonabusive drinking or drug-taking.

Like hypnosis, marijuana and small to moderate amounts of alcohol enhance primary suggestibility. It appears that being a "little high" from either drug pro-duces a state of mind similar to trance. Hypnotic treatment of this habit consists, therefore, of substituting trance for moderate drinking or pot smoking.

Because the state of hypnosis can so accurately mimic being high, in trance, the patient can imagine himself as having just had a drink or smoked one joint. The therapist can even suggest that this state of mild euphoria will remain after the formal trance has ended.

An advantage of using hypnosis rather than drinking or smoking pot is that the trance can be ended quickly and at will rather than having to wait for the length of time it takes for the body to metabolize alcohol or cannabis. Hypnosis would allow a person to go to a party and drink several tall glasses of ginger ale on the rocks. With each drink, this individual would feel a little more tipsy, fitting in with the other partygoers. However, when the party was over, such a person could drive home perfectly soberly.

Fingernail Biting and Related Habits

There are a number of habits that help people relax or discharge tension and that are carried out almost unconsciously. They include fingernail biting, hair pulling (pillapullamania), pulling out eyelashes, and a host of varied tics and nervous habits such as lip biting, thumb sucking, teeth grinding (bruxism), playing with one's hair, and knuckle cracking. Although these complaints may seem trivial or laughable, some people seek assistance with fingertips so raw and bloody that they cannot use their hands. Others come in with only fuzz left on their heads, occasionally wearing wigs that have similarly been denuded. For them, this is a serious complaint indeed.

Hypnotic treatment strategies for such complaints are designed to work only on the behavior itself, not on the underlying motivation. If hair pulling, for example, stems from a severe depression and consequent urge toward self-disfigurement, hypnosis may help control the act, but the more basic problem must await psychotherapy.

A Case of Severe Nail Biting

Mr. Thompson was a forty-year-old father of three who came seeking help with a lifelong habit of biting his nails down to the quick. After taking his history, Dr. Arnold found him to be an intelligent and successful man who worked as the head librarian at a major university. She felt that he exhibited no severe underlying pathology but seemed to be a rather nervous man.

Mr. Thompson was not interested in exploring his tension and its sources. Thus, Dr. Arnold agreed simply to teach him to use hypnosis to help control the urge to bite his nails.

First he was taught to enter a state of hypnosis in the usual fashion. His degree of response was rated, roughly, as in the lower range, though workable. Once hypnosis had been induced, Dr. Arnold said:

While you are feeling so comfortably relaxed, listening effortlessly to my voice, I am going to help you increase

179

your control over your nail biting. Consciously, you really wish to stop biting your nails. Often, however, nail biting begins without conscious awareness on your part. In order for your conscious mind, which wants to stop biting your nails, to exert its influence over your behavior, it has to know about it. When it knows what your hand is doing, it can bring your hand down. Therefore, the first part of our approach will be to increase your awareness of the habit.

You know that putting awful-tasting substances such as quinine on your nails cannot really stop you, but can make you aware of your finger in your mouth. In a moment, I am going to ask you to bring your hand up from the arm of the chair toward your mouth. As you do, you will become aware of a signal. I do not know what it is, and neither do you. However, you will experience a signal that will alert you. [A different, more directive therapist might have ordered a very specific signal.] *Perhaps a buzzing or ringing sound will occur in your brain and grow louder as your hand rises. Perhaps your hand will begin to tingle as though an electric current were running through it. Perhaps a light will flash at the periphery of your vision. Whatever the signal, you just note it and realize that it is telling you that you are in danger of hurting your nails.* [This theme of alertness is then expanded upon.]

That's right, become alert and aware of the fact that you are bringing your fingers toward your mouth. And you know you do not truly want to do this. Your presence here today shows me that.

But it makes you nervous not to carry out the habit-

ual action. Sometimes, you know what you are doing, want to stop it, but feel so tense when you do not let yourself chew on your nails that you decide to give in to the urge. Using this exercise will not only help you to become aware of what you are doing, but will also help by relaxing you. Notice how relaxed you feel. You will not only experience the signal as a warning that your hands are dangerously approaching your face, but will also associate the signal with the sense of deep and comfortable relaxation you now feel. That's right, the signal not only warns you, it tells your body to remember how it feels now.

Further, if a time comes when you are feeling the urge to bite and the signal does not relax you enough, you can do something more than choose between biting nails or sitting and suffering. You can choose to go through the hypnotic exercise to become so relaxed that you will be able to leave your fingers in peace easily.

As an adequate amount had been done for a session, Dr. Arnold reviewed what had been taught and told Mr. Thompson to practice. He was to return in a week.

In their next session Dr. Arnold proceeded:

Think about your hands and your fingers, how they are an integral part of your body. Think about how much you like yourself and you wouldn't want to hurt your body. Picture a dark room. You are being held prisoner there. You've been captured by the Gestapo. They are going to torture you to make you talk. And they are doing it in the classic way. They are going to pull out your fingernails. The officer has found a spot on a finger-

*nail where he can get a grip. He doesn't have his pliers
with him, so he is going to use his teeth to rip your fingernail off and leave the bleeding pulp exposed. Hear yourself scream in agony. Feel the lightning bolts of pain jolt
up your arm. You wish you could do something to make
that torturer stop.*

*Now, pull your attention from the burning throb of
your mutilated finger and look at the Gestapo agent. In
the dim light you see, to your horror, that the face is your
own. Tears come to your eyes as you realize how you have
been hurting yourself.*

Dr. Arnold paused a moment, then continued:

*Now let's switch the scene. I'd like you to focus on your
hand, and as you do, it seems to become less and less a
part of you. You know that when you bite your nails, you
are not really letting yourself be aware that that is your
hand. Let's go a little further. A hand is before you.
Imagine that it belongs to a stable worker. It is your job
to bite the fingernails on it. Go ahead, jam that finger
into your mouth, and begin to chew at the nail. You got
a piece off. Now feel it getting stuck in your gums. Try
not to think what that finger has been doing lately. And
what kind of matter has been collecting under the nails.
Ignore the smell of stable that lingers. Now take another
fingernail. Bite it off; now try to swallow it. Feel it as it
gets stuck in your throat. Feel yourself gag.*

*This nail biting isn't really such a nice habit, is it?
When you find yourself thinking about biting your nails,
you are going to be reminded of the Gestapo agent tor-*

182

*turing you, and of having to bite the nails of a dirty
stranger. As you do, you will realize how much you don't
want to continue this habit. It disgusts you. When that
happens, don't stop there, because the disgust will make
you feel so bad you might want to bite your nails. Instead, go on to think about how it is not too late. Feel
your nails as they begin working to restore strength and
health. Feel the sensation of their growing ever so slowly.
Feel the healing process. Feel good about yourself because
you are going to continue to take good care of yourself.
You can forgive yourself for what you have done, and
there is no need to punish yourself by further nail biting.
It is in your past, and you can go on to let your nails
grow.*

The doctor concluded the second session at this point.

In the third session, Dr. Arnold and Mr. Thompson
talked about specific situations in which he had had trouble controlling the urge to bite his nails. Especially difficult were times when he was reading a book, when he
was sitting at a meeting, and when he noticed the corners
of a nail beginning to grow out. In trance, therefore,
suggestions were made to focus on each of these situations.

*Your long-time habit has been to read a book and chew
on your fingernails. Today we are going to begin to work
especially on that. Imagine yourself holding a book. Feel
your fingers on the book, and feel your fingers becoming
almost a part of the book. Feel how difficult it might be
to pull your fingers off the book. It is as though your fin-*

gers are magnets and the book a piece of iron. You are strong enough to let go long enough to turn the page, but then your fingers are immediately drawn back to the book. As you read, you find it ever so much easier to allow the magnets to hold your fingers on the book.

Next, let's work on being at a meeting. As you sit there, I would like you to let your hands come together and interlock your fingers. Interlock your fingers tightly together. Your fingers are as though they are in Chinese handcuffs. If you relax your fingers, they will sit there quite comfortably. But if you try to pull them apart, pressure will hold them together. You can relax with your fingers intertwined, but if you try to pull them apart, they will resist and hold themselves together. You can sit relaxed at the meeting with your hands at peace, or you can express your tension by letting your hands do isometric exercises, pulling against their tight lock.

Now for our final focus. When you become aware of a corner of a new nail, sometimes you don't really want to bite it, but you want to even it off. You are afraid it may snag and rip. Because of past damage, it is probably growing unevenly. What you should do, though, is realize that using your teeth is not the proper way to manicure your fingernails. Always carry a pocket nail file. If you discover a ragged edge or an uneven spot that needs attention, feel free to take out your file and properly groom that nail. In time you will be able to wait for a socially proper moment to do so, but for the present manicure your nails whenever you feel they need it. You are going to take good care of them.

Mr. Thompson and Dr. Arnold met several more times to refine and personalize the techniques taught during these first three sessions.

Sample Exercise for Hair Pulling

One special problem comes up in habits such as hair or eyelash pulling. It seems as though patients feel there are so many hairs that pulling one or two won't hurt. One technique in such cases is for the patient to imagine himself walking in a garden. He can be instructed as follows:

> *Imagine a large, beautiful flower garden. Pull down and pluck one petal. Pluck another. And another. It won't matter. . . . Look around and see that you've managed to defoliate the entire area. You've ruined this beautiful garden. Realize that's what you've done to yourself, one hair at a time.*

Bedwetting

A great many children continue to wet their beds beyond the age of toilet training. For some, a wet bed greets them every morning; for others, it is a more sporadic but not infrequent occurrence. There are a variety of treatment approaches used for bedwetting (enuresis). Antidepressant medication has proved helpful, possibly because it produces a mild tendency toward urinary retention. Moisture-sensing devices can be used to trigger bells or electric shocks with the first drops of urine. Another approach involves humiliation and ridicule, which produce bad feelings but are not very good at changing behavior. Finally, there are commonsense measures, such as giving no liquids two hours before bedtime, waking up the child and bringing him to the bathroom, or having him use the toilet right before going to sleep.

Hypnosis tends to work well, doubtless in part because it gives the child the opportunity to speak to an understanding, hope-inducing adult. Hypnotic strategies usually focus on awareness and practice. Awareness of bladder condition can be enhanced, for example, by imagining a gauge that indicates bladder fullness. When it is two-thirds full, a "buzzer" might sound. It is important to set the signal at less than maximum capacity lest the sleeper wake up having to urinate so badly that he can't wait. The practice element would typically involve imagining waking up, going to the bathroom, and feeling good waking up in a dry bed.

Teeth Grinding

Teeth grinding (bruxism) is a habit related to tension discharge. Sometimes the regular use of hypnosis to relax reduces or eliminates the problem. Sometimes it needs direct attention. One nice way of treating bruxism is to hypnotize the patient and have him imagine a wonderful scene and smile with pleasure at the thought. He is then instructed to make an association between the sensation of touching his teeth and the pleasant thought that produces a smile. No one can smile and gnash his teeth simultaneously.

In Summary

There are some basic principles and approaches that are common to the treatment of these kinds of habits. Because so often the behavior occurs automatically, with no conscious thought, the first step in curing the habit is to make the patient consciously aware of whatever action it involves. Only when heightened awareness is accomplished can the conscious decision to stop the habit be brought into play. Second, since these habits often serve as a means of tension reduction, an alternative method of relaxation is supplied. Finally, the self-destructive aspects of the habit must be experienced and acknowledged. Before treatment they have necessarily been denied or supressed. Thus, often a third strategy is to make it impossible for the patient to continue ignoring the damage caused by the habit.

Part III
Hypnosis and Medicine

If it is true, as it seems to be, that the human central nervous system can figure out how to . . . instruct its blood vessels, lymphocytes, and heaven knows what other participants in the tissues to eliminate a wart, then it is clear that the human nervous system has already evolved a vast distance beyond medical science. If I had a good wart I'd be happy to be a participant in this experiment. . . . If it worked I would feel gratified by the skill, excessively vain, and ready to dine out forever on the news that my own mind is so much smarter than I am.

Lewis Thomas, M.D., 1983

The chief phenomena [of hypnosis] are indisputable and we ourselves are witness to them; and in it wounds give no pain. In the name therefore of the love of truth, in the name of the dignity of our profession, in the name of the good of all mankind, I implore you carefully to investigate this important subject.

John Elliotson, M.D., 1846

9
Control of Pain

In prehistoric times, when painkillers were not available, a capacity for trance would probably have been most adaptive. Today, even when there are alternatives to hypnosis, trance continues to hold a place as a valuable remedy for pain.

In recent years, research has shown that the body can react to pain by producing naturally occurring, morphinelike substances known as endorphins. These internally produced drugs block reception of painful nerve impulses. When a drug that counteracts their effect is given to people in a trance, even very good hypnotic subjects may find themselves suddenly unable to control pain. This experimental phenomenon seems to indicate that hypnosis can also cause the release of these natural painkillers. How this happens, however, is still not clear.

Hypnosis has a number of aspects that make it appealing as an anesthetic, including an absence of dangerous side effects. For people of extreme hypnotizability, trance can provide total pain relief, the equal of any chemical in effectiveness. Individuals who are average subjects experience a great deal of relief, and even people whose capacity for hypnosis is nonexistent derive some benefits from the relaxation that usually accompanies trance.

The unique selective capacity of hypnosis makes it possible to block out the sensation of pain while simultaneously permitting experience of other, more desirable sensations. For example, cesarean sections can be done with only hypnosis for anesthesia. During these operations the mother feels no discomfort. She is aware, however, of the sensation of the baby being lifted out and can experience the first sight of her newborn.

Pain serves a purpose in carrying a warning that damage is being done to the body. This signal tells the central nervous system to remove the body from the damaging situation or to get help to cure the problem. However, pain frequently persists even when a person knows all about the cause of pain and is taking good care of his body. At this point the pain has outlived its usefulness. People suffering from cancer, for example, often continue to experience pain long after the illness has been diagnosed and proper treatment started. These people are not doing anything that they had best avoid, but the now useless, painful input continues regardless.

Not only can hypnosis relieve functionless, chronic pain, it can do so without resulting in increased vulnerability to accident. A man with unremitting hand pain could, for instance, be cured of his condition by having the relevant nerve or nerves severed. However, along with his chronic discomfort would go all functional pain, all hurt that could act as a warning signal. The inability to feel pain in this limb is potentially dangerous: the hand may be unwittingly badly burned or deeply cut. Since there is no sensation in his hand, this man's reflexive reaction is gone, and his self-injury may continue until he smells a burn, sees blood, or is told that he is hurting himself.

Along the same lines, an athlete suffering from a bruised foot could take a shot of Novocain to deaden the pain so that he could play a game. He then might break a bone in that foot without knowing it and continue to play on a seriously injured foot. With hypnosis, he could dull or eliminate awareness of the painful bruise but leave his nervous system unimpaired in its ability to carry new information of damage to his brain.

The perception of pain involves two components. First of all, there is a sensation of something happening to a specific part of the body. This awareness is purely informational. Second, pain includes a reaction to the information. Thus, in another part of the brain, the limbic system, the "hurt" is added. Instead of being a simple perception, pain takes on emotional impact.

Hypnotic approaches to pain control are based on these two aspects of perception. Hypnosis can be used to block perception of the informational sensation. It can also be used to strip a perception of its emotional impact. Although the distinctions are worth remembering, in practice these two approaches are usually blended. The warning function of pain should be respected, and hypnotic pain control should never be attempted until it is certain that the pain has been correctly diagnosed. The therapist can then offer the patient a whole variety of techniques from which to select the most helpful. The strategies that follow are applicable to any *physically* based pain.

A Case of Phantom Limb Pain

Joe Brooks was a Vietnam veteran who had lost the lower part of his left leg when he stepped on a mine. His rehabilitation had gone quite well, and he had learned to walk with a prosthesis. Joe's emotional response to his loss of limb was considered excellent by the doctors at the Veterans Administration Hospital. Following discharge from the hospital, he had married and gone to work as a cab driver. In spite of his otherwise good adjustment, however, Joe was extremely troubled by phantom limb pain. This kind of pain is a common phenomenon involving misfunction of nerves once connected to a now-missing limb. These nerves continue to send messages to the brain. Sometimes the information relayed is relatively benign, as when the resulting feeling is an itch. At other times it can be excruciating pain.

Joe's pain was frequently severe enough to prevent him from working and sleeping. As is true of many victims of chronic pain, the unrelenting discomfort began to take its toll in his personality, depressing him and making him irritable. (It is important to note that in spite of the depression that often accompanies it, phantom limb pain is not a psychologically caused pain but a physical sensation caused by damaged nerve fibers.)

Joe had been taking codeine to deal with his discomfort. It provided some relief, but less than he felt he

194

needed. Additionally, he did not like the drugged feeling he got from these pills. Wishing to try something else, Joe was referred to the pain clinic of a general hospital. There, a Dr. Hamilton suggested hypnosis as a treatment. Joe found it appealing because he could do it himself, and its efficacy did not decrease over time, unlike that of drugs, to which a tolerance is developed. Furthermore, there were no unpleasant side effects.

On a test of hypnotizability, Joe rated in the high average range. He therefore easily learned the initial step of self-hypnosis for relaxation. (The rationale here is two-fold. People can best handle the fright involved with pain from a relaxed standpoint. Also, tensing muscles speeds up and enhances nerve conduction, which in turn increases pain.)

Dr. Hamilton next taught Joe to float off to a "very nice place," leaving behind the painful body. (People using morphine for pain control often describe a feeling of being at the end of a long tunnel while their body is at the other end. The pain is not blocked but instead seems far away, so that it is almost irrelevant. This kind of dissociative sense is quite easily attained with hypnosis.) Joe accomplished this mental separation by imagining himself lying on a beach, watching a sea gull land. Focusing on the bird, he felt himself more and more *becoming* the gull. Finally, he *was* the gull, which flew away, leaving his painful body behind. (A variation of this technique is to feel or see oneself leaving the body, just as old movies used to show the person's spirit emerging from his motionless body. The person would then feel fine, fit, and healthy. He would see his painful body where he had left it. He would be aware of it and of the experiences it was suffering, but it would be a distant awareness, like that of a surgeon who knows what is going on in the body he is operating on.)

Dr. Hamilton told Joe that sometimes a person can have that healthy, pain-free self go away and then return to a less painful body. The suggestion given is that the sensation of pain is going to have to hunt to catch up with the self, like a letter trying to catch up with someone who has moved frequently. By the time the painful sensation reaches the person who has now returned to his body, it is so worn out from chasing that there is very little pain left.

In their next session, Dr. Hamilton and Joe talked about how Joe had grown so accustomed to the presence of pain that it now was like an old friend or enemy. His discomfort seemed so embedded in his experience that he believed at some level that the pain would never go away. Therefore, Dr. Hamilton said, they would approach the problem of Joe's old pain by introducing a new pain that could be cured. Joe was taught to produce this new pain by pinching with one hand the webbing between the thumb and index finger of his other hand. (This pinching results in a very sharp, intense pain that ceases almost immediately upon release.) Because this discomfort could be easily and quickly stopped, Joe was able to experience a pain he need not fear.

Dr. Hamilton then told Joe that not only would nonpinching stop this temporary hand pain, but also that hypnosis could relieve it. Joe mentioned at this point that he thought hypnosis could only cure psychological pain. Dr. Hamilton assured him that this common impression was false. In fact, the doctor explained, hypnosis was not terribly effective for pain that was truly "all in the head." (Patients sometimes fear that if trance cures, it proves the presence of malingering. They are reassured to learn that hypnosis actually works best on physically based pain.) Thus, one intent in using suggestions to relieve the pinching pain was to convince Joe that hypnosis really could cure physical discomfort. A successful demonstration should then leave him more confident to try hypnosis on his chronic pain.

Accordingly, Dr. Hamilton told Joe to rate the pain produced by pinching his hand on a scale from one to ten. Joe rated it a seven. Dr. Hamilton had him vividly visualize this number. He then suggested to Joe that the number *was* the degree of pain. The number visualized was not only like a thermometer that recorded the event, but also influenced it. When the degree of pain changed, the number changed, and when the number changed, the amount of pain changed. He then instructed Joe to make the number an eight, to see the eight, and to feel the pain of the pinch get worse. (To have told Joe initially to lower the number could easily have seemed like telling him, "Just make the pain go away." Asking him to increase the number and pain, which Joe could do, did not come up against a basic disbelief in the chance of relief.) When Joe was able to increase the amount of pain felt and to "see" the higher number, Dr. Hamilton suggested that Joe now lower the number and feel the pain decrease along with it. Joe was told that he would always be able to see the number associated with the pain he felt and that he could change that number to change the pain. The secret was in vividly seeing the number.

In their third session. Dr. Hamilton and Joe agreed to try a number of different tactics for pain control. All of these variations were to be tried on the pain Joe produced by pinching his hand. Joe was told that not all of the suggestions would work equally well. However, he need not worry about any single one failing, because they would go through quite a long list of possible techniques. Dr. Hamilton instructed Joe that while trying each of these possible exercises, he was also to pinch his hand and rate the pain from zero to ten. Thus Joe would be able to discover for himself which techniques worked best.

They started by reviewing the previously taught out-of-body exercise. Joe rated the pain as zero. He derived a lot of confidence from the fact that he could, with this method, eliminate pain at any time. Both Joe and the doctor agreed that this was not a practical solution for times when Joe needed to be active, however. They then turned their attention to the new exercises.

Joe was told to say the alphabet, focusing on the shape of each letter. He noted that directing attention away from the source of pain lessened it. Joe suggested that he might be able to use such a focusing method while he worked. He could visualize a map of the city and trace the route he would take for his fares.

For the next exercise on the list, Joe was told to experience a tingling in his hand, especially in the tips of his fingers. He was then to touch the webbing of his other hand with these tingling fingers and to transfer the tingle from the fingertips to the webbing. Dr. Hamilton suggested that while the tingling sensation was carried through the nerves, there simply was not enough room for the painful feelings to go through. The prickly feeling was stronger than the pain. Once the tingle was firmly established in the webbing, Joe was to pinch it.

As they continued their fourth session, Joe was told once again to put a tingling feeling into his fingertips. Then he was to bring it up to the back of his neck, finally transferring the sensation into his neck and spine. Dr. Hamilton then suggested to Joe that he feel his spinal cord seeming to fluff up and be transformed from a tight wire to something resembling cotton candy. He would be able to feel or perhaps even see nerve impulses coming through the spine. Joe was then taught three exercises based on this distortion. First, he was told that he could have this area act as a filter, taking out the hurt from the pain. The sensory information could continue, but it would not carry an emotional impact.

Next it was suggested that as the electrical impulses of nerve conduction came through this area, they would not quickly travel through a tight spinal cord but would diffuse. Joe could perceive the nerve impulses meandering through the maze, losing their speed and harshness of impact. When they had passed through, the impulses would continue to the brain but would arrive slowly and softly. Joe would not feel the hard impact of pain. There would be no surprising jolt because Joe would have seen the impulse coming and would have prepared for it.

Dr. Hamilton continued by suggesting that Joe use this area in his spine as a clearinghouse or switchboard.

You know, Joe, that your body is constantly receiving many signals of which you are not consciously aware. For example, if you so direct your attention, you can feel your wristwatch on your wrist. And now that I mention it, you can feel the shoe on your right foot. You can feel it, but you are not aware of it until you direct your attention to it. Part of your brain receives all the signals from your nerves and decides which ones to send through. The others never reach consciousness. Your brain has been confused by the painful messages that have been sent, whether from your hand or your phantom limb. Your brain has been thinking that this pain is a warning or danger signal and should be attended to. However, we both know that there is nothing dangerous about pinching the webbing of your hand, and there is nothing wrong with your left leg that hasn't already been well cared for. There is no useful information here. You are going to be able, now, to filter out those perceptions which carry no worthwhile information for you. As a sensation arrives from pinching your hand, or from your phantom limb, the base of your brain will be able to say, "This is not useful information. There is no need to send this along." Now, obviously, if some different sensation came from your hand or left leg, it would be sent along. But messages of the same pains need not be passed along to consciousness any more than you need to be reminded constantly that you are wearing a watch.

In their final session, Dr. Hamilton taught Joe two related techniques. First, Joe was told to imagine dipping his hand into a bucket of ice water. He felt the hand become colder and colder, until finally it was numb. When it was thoroughly numbed, Joe was to pinch it, feeling nothing. Second, Joe was to imagine Novocain being shot into his wrist, numbing the entire hand.

Next, the effects of relaxation and tension were demonstrated. Joe was told to tense the muscles of his body and pinch his hand. Then he relaxed while repeating the pinch. The second pinch was much less painful.

The following technique surprised and frightened Joe. He was told to pinch his hand, letting all of his attention flow into the pinched area. "That's right. Focus all your attention on that area," said Dr. Hamilton.

You've run from the pain in the past. Now run to it. Feel every exquisite sensation. Feel exactly what is being felt in your hand. Notice every throb, ache, pain. As you do, you find that while it is not beautiful, it is not as frightening as you had imagined. People instinctively run from pain. Even if they cannot escape, they do not stop trying to flee. You carry your pain even when you try to escape from it. The attempt to escape reinforces the idea that it is frightening and must be run away from. As you look closely at it, you can see that it is unpleasant, but not more than you can manage. In fact, you have learned to deal very well with the loss of your leg. You have been able to face that painful fact. You can similarly stare close up at this pain and find it is not bigger than you. It hurts, but it does not frighten.

The final technique Joe learned was to imagine that his left leg was intact. Doing so, he was told to describe the pain. Joe said it was a burning feeling on the bottom of his foot. He was then instructed to place a nice cool cloth on the sole of his foot, or to rub in a cooling lotion that would make the foot better. Dr. Hamilton suggested Joe could help himself by imaging the foot as there and doing whatever would be required to make that imaginary foot feel right.

Joe was well motivated and practiced his techniques faithfully. He found one or two of them to be of so little value that he never bothered with them again. He used all of the rest at various times, learning which was particularly well suited for each different situation. Like many people, the two he found most useful were "filter out useless information from the switchboard" and "get close to and look at the pain."

10
Medical Uses of Hypnosis

The "mysterious leap" from mind to body has long been a source of fascination and puzzlement to healers. Cures swing from one extreme to the other, as first mind, then body is emphasized. In some cultures, magic, the devil, or malevolent other spiritual force is credited as the root of all illness. In others, people have tried to treat the body as an independent entity, firing "magic bullets" at microbes and bacteria. For them the mind is an unfortunate bit of baggage that the patient insists on carrying along.

In thinking about this relationship, two basic statements can be made. First, both mind and body are facets of an individual. What affects one affects the other. Second, nobody really knows for sure just how this interaction works.

There are many ways of influencing the mind through the body or the body through the mind. Hypnosis is a structure for helping a person build a small bridge across the mysterious divide.

A host of physical problems are candidates for hypnosis. Treatment for all of these conditions starts with learning self-hypnosis and, for most, relaxation, then moves on to suggestions tailored to the specific difficulty.

Insomnia

Disturbed patterns of sleep are a common occurrence and a frequent reason for visits to a doctor. This symptom can have a variety of sources. Transient stress, severe depression, poor sleep habits, and physical illness can all effect the quantity and quality of sleep. Drugs such as Valium, Dalmane, chloral hydrate, and barbiturates, which are often used to treat insomnia, have many disadvantages. Some are addictive, and all supress REM (rapid eye movement, or dreaming) sleep, and tend to lose effectiveness over time. Hypnosis has none of these drawbacks yet can still provide symptomatic relief.

Since its early days, hypnosis has been confused with sleep. While hypnosis itself is not like sleep, the state of *falling* asleep – the transition from awake to asleep – is related to a hypnotic state. Frequently people who are using hypnosis for various purposes will find themselves falling asleep. Thus it is not surprising that hypnosis is often successfully used to treat insomnia.

The two main hypnotic strategies for treating this sleep disorder take into account known principles about falling asleep. For example, people who are troubled by insomnia do better if they do not go to bed until they are ready for sleep. In this way bed is not associated with wakeful activity. Also, one cannot expect to be stimulated and drop immediately into slumber.

The first method of dealing with insomnia is to induce trance and suggest a growing sense of sleepiness. This sense can be enhanced by a variety of techniques, including such traditional ones as watching sheep jump-

204

ing over a fence or counting backward from one hundred. As the insomniac becomes more bored and drowsy, he could terminate hypnosis with the final suggestion that as soon as his head hits the pillow, he would be asleep, or he could simply drift from hypnosis into sleep.

It should be remembered that sleep functions as a natural antidote to hypnosis. When a person falls asleep, whether from hypnosis or the usual waking state, he is shifting from one state of consciousness to another. When coming out of sleep, one naturally goes to the usual waking state. People do not wake up hypnotized any more than they wake up asleep.

The familiar thought "If I don't fall asleep, I am going to be tired in the morning" is a common enemy of sleep. Fear of insomnia is a wonderful way of producing it. Understood as a kind of performance anxiety, this fear can be helped by the loosening of rigid standards. For insomnia, the solution lies in making sleep irrelevant. There are two functions to be carried out during sleep, the first being to dream. The amount of sleep involved in this process takes very little time and is essentially unavoidable. Even people fighting to stay awake doze long enough to dream. The other function of sleep is to allow the body to do its "housecleaning." During the day, muscles produce waste products faster than the bloodstream can carry them away. Just as an office building is cleaned at night, while there are fewer workers making more mess, the body carries away lactic acid during sleep, when the muscles are at rest.

People in the state of hypnosis are capable of extreme muscular relaxation. In fact, the degree of relaxation is quite similar to that of sleep. Therefore, if a person sub-stitutes a solid eight hours of hypnosis for sleep, with a brief period of dreaming, he will awake the next morning nearly as refreshed as if he had been asleep.

Hypnotic instructions, then, are to get into bed, enter a state of self-hypnosis, and float off to a nice place. The insomniac is told that his task is to stay peacefully and comfortably relaxed in that pleasant scene. If he falls asleep, that is fine. If he wakes up in the middle of the night, he is to reinduce hypnosis immediately and return to his pleasant scene. If he does not fall asleep, that is not a problem, because his body is relaxed.

A difficulty in this set of instructions is resisting the temptation to ruminate and focus on worries, real or imagined. The technique of sorting and mentally flagging thoughts can then be helpful. After surveying the ideas clamoring for attention, the insomniac can decide there is nothing he need do except sleep or relax, with all attention focused on a peaceful scene.

Migraine Headaches

When the veins that normally allow blood to leave the head become constricted, buildup of excess blood in the head results in a migraine. A simple but effective treat-ment to remove this extra blood is for the sufferer to imagine a scene involving extremes of heat and cold. One could be directed to imagine, for instance, sitting in front of a roaring fireplace on a cold night. Feet and hands are held close to the fire's radiant warmth. The head, how-ever, is leaning against the cold, drafty window. The hypnotic suggestion given is that, just as these variations in temperature are vividly experienced, so will there be shifts in the temperature of different parts of the body. The hands and feet will be warmed as more blood flows to them. The head will cool off as blood leaves it. The effect is to cure the migraine. This technique also works well for a person whose poor circulation causes chronic cold extremities.

For some people, other images involving the free flow of blood are helpful. Visualizing a valve that controls the flow of blood through the veins gives a means of opening up the constricted veins. Some people can even visualize tight veins loosening and dilating.

High Blood Pressure

High blood pressure has been easily and successfully treated with hypnosis. People with hypertension who enter a relaxed hypnotic trance twice daily for twenty minutes at a time develop decreased blood pressure. The effect is not limited solely to the time spent in trance, but it lasts all day. The change is not irreversible, however. When the daily practice is stopped, blood pressure goes back up.

Bleeding

Even moderately hypnotizable people can demonstrate startling control of bleeding. Many people are able to constrict the flow of blood through the capillaries, sometimes to the point that even if scratched, they do not bleed a drop. The usual hypnotic suggestions for decreasing blood flow are of coldness of the skin, tourniquetlike pressure, numbness, or even that the skin is leather coating rather than living tissue.

For deeper wounds or larger blood vessels, the quantity of blood lost, as well as the rate of clotting, can be changed. Commonly, a moderately hypnotizable person who has a vein pierced can reduce by half the amount of time it takes for the bleeding to stop. The quantity of blood lost is similarly decreased. The suggestions used include those for lesser wounds as well as introducing the ideas of feeling the wound close, feeling the blood thicken and form a scab, or imagining a gauzy net forming to catch the blood cells as an aid to coagulation. These suggestions have even been used successfully with hemophiliacs, allowing them both to undergo optional surgical procedures and to control internal or accidental bleeding.

Warts

It is known that common warts are caused by a virus, that they grow singly or in clusters, that they remain for totally unpredictable lengths of time, and that they may spontaneously disappear altogether.

Doctors have treated warts with a variety of procedures, including freezing the area with liquid nitrogen, repeatedly applying acid, and cutting the wart out surgically. Sometimes after such treatment the wart will not reappear. Sometimes a new one will grow in the old one's place. Folk remedies for warts abound, and, interestingly enough, these outlandish cures sometimes work quite well.

The human body has the capacity to combat the wart-causing virus. It just needs somehow to be told to do so. Hypnosis is one such possible way. The enhanced link between mind and body that occurs during hypnosis allows the message to go through. However, because it is not clear exactly how the body acts to destroy the virus, it is difficult to give the body explicit directions on what steps it must take to rid itself of warts. That is, unlike migraine headaches, where it is known that extra blood in the head causes painful pressure, and which therefore respond well to the hypnotic imagery of blood moving out of the head and into the hands and feet, warts cannot be eliminated by the use of a hypnotic image that exactly mimics the body's physical defense. Consequently, hypnotic treatment of warts essentially consists of the command "Body, heal yourself, however you do it" and a suggestion to the patient that he visualize replacement of the warts by new, healthy skin.

Psoriasis

Psoriasis and similar skin conditions tend to get better in the summertime when the sufferer can go to the beach and expose the diseased skin to warm, dry heat. One hypnotic approach to psoriasis, therefore, is to have the patient imagine lying in the sun, focusing on the sensation of the heat of the sun's rays. This imaginal sunbath in fact produces an increase in skin temperature due to blood flow. The effect is a drying of the skin and an improvement in the psoriasis.

A variant technique was created by a patient who had experienced the healing effects of bathing in the mineral-rich Dead Sea. She imagined herself floating in this water, feeling the healing salts on her skin. The result was a marked improvement in her condition.

Severe Morning Sickness

A certain amount of queasiness or morning sickness is traditionally associated with pregnancy. As the body's metabolism tries to adjust to the hormonal changes, a vitamin deficiency frequently occurs which results in a sensation of nausea or vomiting. For some women, however, the symptoms do not end after the first trimester. Their symptoms (known as hyperemesis gravidarum) can become so severe that there is not only discomfort but even pregnancy-threatening weight loss. In some cases, abortion may become necessary, even with women who have had to work very hard to become pregnant in the first place.

Like phobias, severe morning sickness seems to involve a capacity for hypnosis gone awry. Women who suffer from this syndrome are above average in hypnotizability, and, not surprisingly, that same capacity is useful in its treatment. When the sense of nausea due to a physical cause is strongly felt, a woman of high hypnotizability may inadvertently learn to imagine vividly the sensation even when the physical cause has disappeared.

Contrary to the frequent assumption, such women are no more ambivalent or unhappy about being pregnant than any other typical group of women.

Hypnotic treatment of hyperemesis tends to be easy. Several techniques can be tried and the woman given her choice of which she likes best. One suggestion is to imagine vividly smelling a fresh lemon. Most people find the scent of lemon a clean smell, the antithesis of nausea. Another technique is to suggest the development of a tingling sensation in the fingers. That feeling is then transferred to the abdomen, where it becomes a generalized, warm sense of comfort and peace. A variant is to have this feeling occur in the throat, relaxing the muscles so much as to effectively paralyze the gag reflex. In more extreme cases, it is sometimes transiently necessary to have the woman imagine floating off to a peaceful scene so that anxiety about using the technique does not interfere.

Chemotherapy Side Effects

For patients with treatable forms of cancer, the side effects of chemotherapy can feel worse than the disease itself. Drugs powerful enough to combat cancer are not well tolerated by the body. Nausea and vomiting are frequent unpleasant side effects.

The approach used for morning sickness translates directly to chemotherapy side effects. In addition, people have been helped by using images that make them feel that they are fighting the cancer cells. For example, some people imagine their white blood cells as powerful white

Siberian huskies roaming as a pack through the body, hunting cancer cells. It should be emphasized that this use of hypnosis is absolutely ineffective in treating the cancer itself. While hypnosis can cure growths such as warts, cancer seems to be so overwhelming that hypnosis is not powerful enough to defeat the disease. However, even though the use of imagery such as the Siberian huskies does not make tumors shrink, it does make people feel better about themselves, less helpless or passive in the face of illness. This positive attitude promotes the will to survive and determination to battle the illness.

Burns

Cases of people in primitive cultures walking barefoot on red-hot coals have been well documented. These fire-walkers clearly enter a trance before their feet ever touch the coals. It seems as if they are then able to direct an increased flow of blood through their feet as well as to increase perspiration, which serves to carry off the excess heat.

In a similar way, laboratory subjects are able to tolerate small burns without blistering. A subject who imagines he is being touched with a pencil, when in fact the touch is made by a red-hot iron, is not hurt and shows no sign of the burn. Conversely, suggestions that a small coin placed on a subject's skin is extremely hot do produce a burn.

It has been found that hypnotic treatment of burn victims as soon after the event as possible, but no longer than twelve to twenty-four hours later, can impressively reduce the amount of blistering and dramatically shorten the healing and recovery process. The usual suggestions given in such cases are to feel coolness and dryness on the burned area rather than having the body react in the usual but not always constructive way, by massive blistering.

A Final Note

Since the power of the hypnotist to help produce change is less than the power of the patient to resist, hypnotic techniques are not always successful. When they do work, however, they can work surprisingly well with none of the side effects of more common or traditional treatments.

Part IV
Hypnosis and the Law

A man's memory may almost become the art of continually varying and misrepresenting his past, according to his interests in the present.

George Santayana

When I was younger I could remember anything, whether it happened or not.

Mark Twain

II
The Nature of Memory

A reporter from a national tabloid sold at grocery check-out counters everywhere contacted a hypnotist on a story. The reporter explained that a man had toured the galaxy on a flying saucer. The authenticity of the flight had been proved because, under hypnosis, the "space traveler" had recalled seeing a star chart that made no sense unless the stars were viewed from a point in space far different from our corner of the galaxy.

The reporter offered the hypnotist the job of rehypnotizing the man to find any previously overlooked juicy details. The only necessary qualification for the job was an academic appointment at a prestigious university. The hypnotist was quite sure that in trance the "space traveler" would be able to provide interesting new bits of information and that his additional testimony would not refute any previous part of his story. As the hypnotist told the reporter, however, neither "remembering" the star chart or any new "facts," nor the storyteller's very strong, unswerving belief in his travels, as revealed under hypnosis, had any bearing on the actual existence of the UFO trip. Thus, despite the more than reasonably generous fee offered, the hypnotist decided he wanted nothing to do with any headline that read "HARVARD PRO-FESSOR CONFIRMS UFO KIDNAPPING WITH HYPNOSIS."

The issues involved in this vignette, the use of trance to enhance memory and confirm remembrances as fact, are the same questions that arise in the rapidly growing field of forensic hypnosis. Since the 1970s, many police forces have trained detectives to use hypnosis. These detective-hypnotists use their talents in investigations, specifically helping eyewitnesses to recover crime-related memories.

Noticing the absence of routine safeguards in such investigative efforts, members of the hypnosis societies (the Society for Clinical and Experimental Hypnosis and the International Society for Hypnosis) have offered expert opinions as to its proper use. These suggestions have been inconsistently accepted by the courts, rendering them law in some states, of no account in others. The experts, in any case, based their advice, opinions, and suggested guidelines for forensic hypnosis on an understanding of the nature of memory.

The process of remembering is perhaps most easily understood in terms of a mechanical metaphor. It is as if all the sensations coming in from the body and going to the brain arrive at an evaluation center that then selects which parts of this input should be recorded and for how long. Most screened information is judged trivial and thus is discarded. The information that is to be retained is recorded on what can be thought of as a very short-term memory tape. This "tape" holds the memories of the last twenty minutes in some detail. As these memories are constantly reviewed, the most important of them are

put onto a medium-term memory tape. The rest are discarded. During sleep, as part of the function of dreaming,
the medium-term tapes are reviewed and the most important parts are put into long-term memory. The rest is
lost. The short- and medium-term memory tapes are
erased and recorded over.

Human memory is not really a simple tape recorder
or computer that correctly retains every detail of every
experience a person has ever had. Some memories are
neither misplaced in the brain nor repressed but are lost
forever because they *never became a part of the long-term
memory bank.*

Unfortunately, there continue to be poorly trained
hypnotists who start with the assumption that every pertinent memory *must* exist in the witness's mind, and
hypnosis is simply a means to retrieve or locate what is
hidden somewhere in the brain. Mistakenly believing in
the presence of a crucial memory, a hypnotist will tend
to push for it. What happens to a motivated subject who
is pressed by a hypnotist to produce information that is
literally not there? He or she *confabulates.* When "I don't
know" is not acceptable, a person will guess. The use of
trance in these kinds of situations produces the false and
misleading impression that guesses are not guesses at all
but are the deepest truth, which has been dredged up
from the mind's computer through the power of hypnosis. A major problem in forensic hypnosis is the continued existence of the mistaken impression that everything said in trance is fact, that all bits of information
garnered from a hypnotized individual are accurate.
Sometimes they are, and sometimes they are not. Some-

times there is an admixture of guesswork, fantasy, and fact.

Memory is subject to a number of influences. Vulnerable to distortion without hypnosis, it becomes more so with hypnosis. The following experiment demonstrates one such distortion. A subject is first asked if he slept soundly the previous night. He says that he did and denies waking up. Next, trance is induced. During hypnosis, the hypnotist starts a dialogue that goes something like this:

H: *Did you sleep well last night?*
S: *Yes.*
H: *Weren't you woken up by the screeching siren of the fire engine going down the street at about two in the morning?*
S: *Yes, I did wake up for that, now that you mention it.*
H: *Do you know what time it was when the fire engine went by?*
S: *It was two-seventeen.*
H: *How do you know that?*
S: *I remember looking over at my digital alarm clock when I heard the fire engine go by.*

Later, out of trance, the subject is likely to recall strongly the fire engine during the night. Either he will not recall that he previously denied waking up, or he will say, "I had forgotten that I woke up." He will also be able to supply reasons for knowing it was a fire engine, not an ambulance or police car. Now, such memory tampering does not work so well if one tries to tell an honest subject to remember a fire truck going by in the middle of the morning, or at any other time the subject was alert and paying attention to what was going on. He is apt to be sure of remembrances made during this time. When memory is hazy or uncertain, however, false memories can easily be inserted.

Most people, hypnotized or unhypnotized, tend to follow leading questions. Good hypnotic subjects are typically quite perceptive of and responsive to even subtle cues given by the hypnotist. When the hypnotist is a detective, working with police officers who lack the evidence to convict, for example, the tall, mustachioed, bald suspect they feel sure is guilty, it is not inconceivable that the hypnotist might (perhaps quite unintentionally) lead a witness to identify that suspect. "Was he a tall guy? Did he have a mustache? Was he bald?" might help an eyewitness to "remember" that the criminal was a tall, mustachioed, bald man. Even questions such as "Did you hear the gunshot?" produce a frame of reference for the subject that is different from that produced by "Did you hear a bang?," ". . . a crash?," ". . . a noise?," ". . . anything?"

Memory is subject to external influences as well as internal ones. It is common for a person who is telling a story to embellish the tale. In the absence of evidence either way, what might have been tends to become what was. The storyteller begins to describe as fact what began as speculation. Also, as all fishermen know, as time passes, details tend to grow or become exaggerated in the mind.

Without willful intent to lie, the teller makes his story more and more interesting, and it is the embellished version that is recalled.

The use of hypnosis as an aid to memory magnifies this human tendency. For most individuals who try to recall an experience, memory is filled with uncertainties and vagaries. A person who uses hypnosis to recall an event will be able to remember very vividly or even relive that event. As he does so, there probably are details that are filled in on the basis of what is likely rather than on total accurate recall. At the end of hypnosis, the person will have, in effect, two memories of the same event. He will have the typical inexact original recollection. He will also remember being hypnotized and recall the reliving of the event in hypnosis. This latter memory will be clearer, sharper, and more real. Subsequently, when asked to recall the event, he will go back, not to the original event, but to the remembrance as experienced in the hypnotic trance. This recollection, however, is one that has been tampered with. The memory is stripped of the uncertainties that otherwise could have been used to point out the areas of nonexistent or vague recall. A witness who has not been hypnotized may say, for instance, "I think this happened." A lawyer hearing "think" rather than "know" will understand the choice of word to indicate that the witness is not totally sure about the happening. The differences in word choice help to distinguish the facts a witness genuinely knows from those which are more speculative.

These areas of uncertainty, together with any indications of doubt, tend to disappear when the person has

222

rehearsed his memory while in a trance. A previously hypnotized witness will, in court, give a clear, confident, straightforward narration of the "facts" with no hesitation or guesswork. He will not be lying or consciously covering up unknowns. He will truly believe in the accuracy of his recall. His self-confidence is compelling, and he becomes a convincing witness precisely because his memory has been tampered with.

12
Hypnosis in the Courtroom

In psychotherapy it does not matter what the exact facts of a patient's memory are. Many times a person will describe a past event that is not historically accurate. The original kernel of fact has been dramatically embellished in the unconscious. The result is a memory that may be historically inexact but that gives a clear and accurate picture of how the patient perceives his past or a particular conflict. These screen memories are rather like fables, telling a greater truth at the expense of fact. A therapist would much prefer to hear a patient's screen memory than invite in outside sources for hard, accurate data.

In therapy, it may not matter whether, for example, the patient as a child was molested by the butler or the chauffeur, but from a legal point of view, it may be a vital issue. If the butler is on trial for statutory rape and the chauffeur really did it, the accuracy of the victim's memory is all-important.

The difference in emphasis can also be seen in the case of a criminal with multiple personality. The criminal may honestly claim he committed the crime while in a fugue state and thus had no awareness of his actions. The task in therapy is to understand and resolve the conflicts that led to the emergence of the extra personalities. A judge's concern, however, is to lock up the guilty body, no matter how many personalities go along with it.

The hypnotic capacity that can produce multiple personalities does not excuse their behavior. The hypnosis that helps a person free up both the capacities to fantasize and to remember in no way helps distinguish the one from the other. While hypnosis is very useful in opening up and increasing the amount of material available to a person, it does not establish whether or not that material is true. Hypnosis changes the balance among what a person knows, doesn't know, and thinks he knows. Hypnosis makes a person more sensitive to the subtle cues of the questioner. Hypnosis allows insertion of false recollection when memory is hazy. Hypnosis makes a subject more confident of his memory while it tampers with the memory itself. In spite of these drawbacks, most reliable authorities agree that hypnosis can be helpful in certain legal situations.

CASES OF HYPNOSIS USED IN CRIMINAL LAW

1. A district attorney sent a woman to a hypnotist in hopes she would be able to identify the men who had kidnapped and gang-raped her. The hypnotist was told certain facts of the case: Several people had seen the woman dragged into a car, which sped off with her. Two days later, police found this car, which was stolen, abandoned near an old factory. The woman was in it, tied and blindfolded. She had obviously been beaten, and there

226

was physical evidence of rape. The woman told the police that her assailants had threatened to kill her if she were to look at them. She had, however, seen them when they first grabbed her as well as on a few occasions when her blindfold slipped.

This woman wanted very much to point out the guilty men, but she remained terrified of doing so. Consequently, she was unable to make any positive identifications.

The hypnotist helped her to relax enough so that her fear would not interfere with memory. Next, she was told that when she thought about the men's appearances, she started with a mental picture. As she transformed the picture into words, much of the important detail was lost. (She did not have a rich and full vocabulary which further limited her descriptions.) She was then instructed to picture the faces – to *see* them, not describe them – so that when she went through the mug shots she could compare the faces in the book to the faces pictured in her memory.

She was able to do so, and her positive identification led the detectives to her assailants. Their fingerprints matched those found in the stolen car. This match, along with other corroborating evidence, eventually resulted in their conviction.

2. A man crossing a street was hit by a car. As the car raced away without stopping, this man clearly saw the license plate. Somewhat dazed, he began repeating the plate number over and over in a singsong fashion. Entering a nearby house, he announced that he had been hit

227

and asked if he could call the police. Still remembering the plate number like a jingle, he asked the phone number of the police and dialed it. As he did so, he realized that he had switched from repeating the plate number to repeating the phone number. While he could remember the make, model, and color of the car, and could accurately describe the driver, he forgot the license number.

He sought help through hypnosis. Specifically told not to try remembering the license, he was instructed in hypnosis to focus on the way he felt as he was entering the house to phone the police. He gradually became aware of the crucial jingle in the back of his mind and then was able to recall the plate number.

3. A small airplane crashed, killing the only passenger and leaving the pilot with no memory at all of the flight. In spite of the many people who saw the crash, and the investigation of the wreckage, the cause of the crash could not be determined. Solely on the strength of the pilot's good reputation, pilot error was not an iron-clad assumption but rather a question. Finally, for his own satisfaction and to satisfy the investigators, the pilot tried hypnosis to lift his amnesia.

He had felt so horrible and guilty about the death of his passenger that he had been previously unable to remember anything about the flight. Now, as the pilot started reliving this flight in trance, he noticed something wrong with the plane. He was not sure what it was but described in detail what was happening to the plane. His detailed account led investigators to suspect carburetor involvement. When they knew specifically where to look, they were able to locate evidence of the carburetor trouble that had caused the crash.

4. The main witness for the prosecution at a murder trial swore positive identification of the defendant. Her hypnotically enhanced identification was later thrown out of court because three clearly established facts – (1) the distance between the eyewitness and the criminal, (2) the lighting conditions, and (3) the power of the human eye – made it *impossible* that she could have perceived more than a blurry smudge, not the extremely detailed, crisp view she reported. This well-meaning witness had produced fantasy and believed it. Without the presence of contrary facts, the jury could easily have believed it as well.

5. A claim of amnesia is often the last resort of people who are caught red-handed. If the police enter a room, find a dead body, and see someone standing over it, holding a smoking pistol in one hand and the deceased's bulging wallet in the other, the guilty party has only one "defense": "I don't know what happened. I can't remember anything."

It is pointless to use hypnosis on this kind of amnesia. An admission – "Now I remember. I thought how nice it would be to have some money and decided to commit armed robbery. When the victim resisted, I shot him" – is no more likely to be forthcoming with hypnosis than without it.

Forensic hypnosis is a young science, and guidelines for its use are continually evolving. Experts tend to agree, however, on certain basic safeguards. Testimony of hypnotized witnesses should not, in and of itself, be considered hard evidence. Hypnosis should rather be thought of as a useful way of generating leads for the police to investigate and corroborate. The hypnosis should be done by an independent psychologist or physician who has appropriate specialized training in forensic hypnosis, not by a police officer. Exactly what the hypnotist is told prior to meeting with the subject should be clearly documented. The information shared with the hypnotist should contain only facts that have been independently established. The subject should be told that hypnosis is not a magical tool that guarantees the production of accurate memories. The hypnotist should be extremely careful not to plant suggestions in the mind of the subject. Finally, and most important, *all* contact between subject and hypnotist should be video-taped so that the inevitable inadvertent cues and leading questions can be spotted later.

The CIA has made the problem of hypnotic memory tampering the focus of some interesting research. The agency has conducted experiments to test the usefulness of hypnosis as a tool in preparing agents for enemy questioning. It was hoped by the researchers that the hypnotic distortion of memory (e.g., insertion of alibi, false background) could make an agent immune to even the most vigorous interrogation.

The desire to use hypnosis in these matters reflects an honest effort to support "justice" in the world. Like-

230

wise, police forces may use hypnosis because they are sincerely and honestly trying to find out who is guilty or innocent, to solve local crimes justly. However, just as those devoted to curing psychological or physical problems must be aware of what hypnosis can and cannot do, and when it should or should not be used, so must agencies and individuals dedicated to law enforcement keep in mind the limitations as well as the potential constructive purposes of forensic hypnosis.

ABOUT THE AUTHORS

SEAN F. KELLY, PH.D., is an Instructor in Psychology in the Department of Psychiatry at the Harvard Medical School. He is a board-certified psychologist on the staff of Beth Israel Hospital in Boston and is in private practice. He has been active in the Society for Clinical and Experimental Hypnosis and is an editorial consultant to the *International Journal of Clinical and Experimental Hypnosis*.

REID J. KELLY, ACSW, is a graduate of Smith College School for Social Work and is a licensed independent clinical social worker. She has worked in several clinical and administrative positions. Reid and Sean Kelly have co-written a number of papers on hypnosis and psychotherapy. They are the parents of two children.

Bibliography

List of Abbreviations

AGP   *Archives of General Psychiatry*
AJP   *American Journal of Psychiatry*
AS   *American Scientist*
IJCEH   *International Journal of Clinical and Experimental Hypnosis*
JAP   *Journal of Abnormal Psychology*
JASP   *Journal of Abnormal and Social Psychology*
JEP   *Journal of Experimental Psychology*
JNMD   *Journal of Nervous and Mental Disorders*
JNP   *Journal of Neuropsychiatry*
JP   *Journal of Psychology*
JPSP   *Journal of Personality and Social Psychology*
PB   *Psychological Bulletin*

Aas, A. Hypnotizability as a function of non-hypnotic experience. *JASP*, 1963, 66, 142–150.

Ault, R. L. Jr. FBI guidelines for use of hypnosis. *IJCEH*, 1979, 27, 449–451.

Barber, T. X. Experimental controls and the phenomena of "hypnosis": A critique of hypnotic research methodology. *JNMD*, 1962, 134, 493–505.

————. *Hypnosis: A scientific approach*. New York: Van Nostrand, 1969.

———— (ed.). *Advances in Altered States of Consciousness and Human Potentialities*, vol. 1. New York: Psychological Dimensions, 1976.

————, and Calverley, D. S. "Hypnotic behavior" as a function of task motivation. *JP*, 1962, 54, 363–389.

————, and Calverley, D. S. Toward a theory of "hypnotic" behavior: Effects on suggestibility of task motivating instructions and attitudes towards hypnosis. *JASP*, 1963, 67, 557–565.

————, and Calverley, D. S. Toward a theory of "hypnotic" behavior: Replication and extension of experiments by Barber and co-workers (1962–65) and Hilgard and Tart (1966). *IJCEH*, 1968, 16, 179–195.

————, and Glass, L. B. Significant factors in hypnotic behavior. *JASP*, 1962, 64, 222–228.

Benson, H.; Arns, P.A.; and Hoffman, J. W. The relaxation response and hypnosis. *IJCEH*, 1981, 29, 259–270.

Bentler, P. M., and Hilgard, E. R. A comparison of group and individual induction of hypnosis with self-scoring and observer-scoring. *IJCEH*, 1963, 11, 49–54.

————, and Roberts, M. R. Hypnotic susceptibility assessed in large groups. *IJCEH*, 1963, 11, 93–97.

Bowers, K. S. *Hypnosis for the Seriously Curious*. Monterey, Calif.: Brooks/Cole, 1976.

Breuer, J., and Freud, S. Studies in hysteria. *The Standard Edition of the Complete Psychological Works of Sig-*

mund Freud, vol. 2. London: Hogarth, 1955.

Carroll, Lewis *Through the Looking-Glass, and What Alice Found There*. New York: Macmillan, 1871.

Case, D. B.; Fogel, D. H.; and Pollack, A. Self-hypnosis and mild hypertension: A study of acute and long-term effects of self-hypnosis on blood pressure. *IJCEH*, 1980, 28, 27–38.

Coe, W. C. Further norms on the Harvard Group Scale of Hypnotic Susceptibility, form A. *IJCEH*, 1964, 12, 184–190.

———, Kobayashi, K.; and Howard, M. L. An approach towards isolating factors that influence antisocial conduct in hypnosis. *IJCEH*, 1972, 20, 118–131.

Cohen, M. E., and Cobb, S. The use of hypnosis in the study of acid-base balance of the blood in a patient with hysterical hyperventilation. *Research Publications of the Association for Nervous and Mental Disorders*, 1939, 19, 318–332.

Conn, J., H. The myth of coercion through hypnosis. *IJCEH*, 1981, 29, 95–100.

Deckert, G. H., and West, L. J. The problem of hypnotizability: A review. *IJCEH*, 1963, 11, 205–235.

Dumas, L. A subjective report of inadvertent hypnosis. *IJCEH*, 1964, 12, 78–86.

DuMaurier, G. *Trilby: A Novel*. New York: Harper, 1894.

Edelstein, M. G. *Trauma, Trance, and Transformation: A Clinical Guide to Hypnotherapy*. New York: Brunner/ Mazel, 1981.

Eisen, M. R., and Fromm, E. The clinical use of self-hypnosis in hypnotherapy: Tapping the functions of imagery and adaptive regression. *IJCEH*, 1983, 31, 243–255.

Elliotson, J. *Harveian Oration*. London: Walton and Mitchell, 1846.

Estabrooks, G. H. *Hypnosis: Current Problems*. New York: Harper and Row, 1962.

Evans, F. J. An experimental indirect technique for the induction of hypnosis without awareness. *IJCEH*, 1967, 15, 72–85.

————. Suggestibility in the normal waking state. *PB*, 1967, 67, 114–129.

————, and Schmeidler, D. Relationship between the Harvard Group Scale of Hypnotic Susceptibility and the Stanford Hypnotic Susceptibility Scale: Form C. *IJCEH*, 1966, 14, 333–343.

Eysenck, H. J. Suggestibility and hypnosis. *JNP*, 1943, 6, 22–31.

————, and Furneaux, W. D. Primary and secondary suggestibility: An experimental and statistical study. *JEP*, 1945, 35, 485–503.

Frank, J. D. *Persuasion and Healing*. Baltimore: Johns Hopkins, 1961.

Frankel, F. H. Trance capacity and the genesis of phobic behavior. *AGP*, 1974, 31, 261–263.

————. *Hypnosis: Trance as a Coping Mechanism*. New York: Plenum, 1976.

————. Hypnosis and related clinical behavior. *AJP*, 1978, 135, 664–668.

————. Hypnosis and hypnotizability scales: A reply. *IJCEH*, 1982, 30, 354–376.

————; Apfel, R.; Kelly, S. F.; Benson, H.; Quinn, T.; Newmark, J.; and Malmaud, R., The use of hypnotizability scales in the clinic: A review after six years. *IJCEH*, 1979, 27, 63–73.

————, and Orne, M. T. Hypnotizability and phobic behavior. *AGP*, 1976, 33, 1259–1261.

Freud, S. Analysis of a phobia in a five year old boy. *The Standard Edition of the Complete Psychological Works of Sigmund Freud*, vol. 10. London: Hogarth, 1955.

————. New introductory lectures on psychoanalysis. *The Standard Edition of the Complete Psychological Works of Sigmund Freud*, vol. 22. London: Hogarth, 1964.

Fromm, E.; Brown, D. P.; Hurt, S. W.; Oberlander, J. Z.; Boxer, A. M.; and Pfiefer, G. The phenomenon and characteristics of self-hypnosis. *IJCEH*, 1981, 29, 189–246.

Fromm, E., and Shor, R. E. *Hypnosis: Research Developments and Perspectives*. Chicago: Aldine, 1972.

Fuchs, K.; Paldi, E.; Abramovici, H.; and Peretz, B. A. Treatment of hyperemesis gravidarum by hypnosis. *IJCEH*, 1980, 28, 313–323.

Gill, M. M., and Brenman, M. *Hypnosis and Related States*. New York: International Universities Press, 1959.

Gordon, J. E. *Handbook of Clinical and Experimental Hypnosis*. New York: Macmillan, 1967.

Haley, J. (ed.). *Advanced Techniques of Hypnosis and Therapy: Selected Papers of Milton H. Erickson, M.D.* New York: Grune and Stratton, 1967.

Hartman, B. J. Self-scoring and observer-scoring estimates of hypnotic susceptibility in a group situation. *Perceptual and Motor Skills*, 1965, 20, 452.

Hilgard, E. R. *Hypnotic Susceptibility*. New York: Harcourt, Brace, and World, 1965.

————. Hypnotic phenomena: The struggle for scientific acceptance. *AS*, 1971, 57, 567–577.

————, and Hilgard, J. R. *Hypnosis in the Relief of Pain*. Los Altos, Calif.: Kaufman, 1975.

————; Lauer, L. W.; and Morgan, A. H. *Manual for Standard Profile Scales of Hypnotic Susceptibility*. Palo Alto: Consulting Psychologists Press, 1963.

————, and Loftus, E. F. Effective interrogation of the eyewitness. *IJCEH*, 1979, 27, 342–357.

————, and Tart, C. T. Responsiveness to suggestions following waking and imagination instructions and following induction of hypnosis. *JAP*, 1966, 71, 196–208.

Hilgard, J. *Personality and Hypnosis*. Chicago: University of Chicago Press, 1970.

Hull, C. L. *Hypnosis and Suggestibility: An Experimental Approach*. New York: Appleton-Century-Crofts, 1933.

Janet, P. *The Major Symptoms of Hysteria*. New York: Macmillan, 1907.

Kelly, S. F. Hypnotizabililty and the inadvertent experi-

ence of pain. *IJCEH*, 1980, 28, 189–191.
————. Measured hypnotic response and phobic behavior. *IJCEH*, 1984, 32, 1–5.
Kleinhauz, M.; Dreyfuss, D. A.; Beran, B.; Goldberg, T.; and Azikri, D. Developments of psychopathological manifestations after participating in stage hypnosis. *IJCEH*, 1979, 27, 219–226.
Kroger, W. S., and Douce, R. G. Hypnosis in criminal investigation. *IJCEH*, 1979, 27, 358–374.
Kroger, W. S., and Fezler, W. D. *Hypnosis and Behavior Modification: Imagery Conditioning*. Philadelphia: Lippincott, 1976.
Kubie, L. S., and Margolin, S. The process of hypnotism and the nature of the hypnotic state. *AJP*, 1944, 100, 611–622.
Kuhner, A. Hypnosis without hypnosis. *IJCEH*, 1962, 10, 93–99.

Levitt, E. E., and Brady, J. P. Muscular endurance under hypnosis and in the waking state. *IJCEH*, 1964, 12, 21–27.
London, P., and Fuhrer, M. Hypnosis, motivation and performance. *Journal of Personality*, 1961, 29, 321–333.

Morgan, A. H., and Hilgard, J. R. Stanford Hypnotic Clinical Scale. In Hilgard and Hilgard, 1975.

O'Connell, D. N. An experimental comparison of hypnotic depth measured by self-ratings and by an objective scale. *IJCEH*, 1964, 12, 34–46.

Orne, M. T. The nature of hypnosis: Artifact and essence. *JASP*, 1959, 58, 277–299.

———. A note on the occurrence of hypnosis without conscious intent. *IJCEH*, 1964, 12, 75–77.

———. Hypnosis, motivation and compliance. *AJP*, 1966, 122, 721–726.

———. Can a hypnotized subject be compelled to carry out otherwise unacceptable behavior? *IJCEH*, 1972, 20, 101–117.

———. The use and misuse of hypnosis in court. *IJCEH*, 1979, 27, 311–341.

———, and Evans, F. J. Social control in the psychological experiment: Anti-social behavior and hypnosis. *JPSP*, 1965, 1, 189–200.

———; Hilgard, E. R.; Spiegel, H.; Spiegel, D.; Crawford, H. J.; Evans, F. J.; Orne, E. C.; and Frischholz, E. J. The relation between the Hypnotic Induction Profile and the Standard Hypnotic Susceptibility Scales, forms A and C. *IJCEH*, 1979, 27, 85–102.

Perry, C. Hypnotic coercion and compliance to it: A review of evidence presented in a legal case. *IJCEH*, 1979, 28, 187–218.

Putnam, W. H. Hypnosis and distortions in eyewitness memory. *IJCEH*, 1979, 27, 437–448.

Rowland, L. W. Will hypnotized persons try to harm themselves or others? *JASP*, 1939, 34, 114–117.

Sanders, R. S., and Reyher, J. Sensory deprivation and

the enhancement of hypnotic susceptibility. *JAP*, 1969, 74, 375–381.

Schafer, D. W., and Rubio, R. Hypnosis to aid the recall of witnesses. *IJCEH*, 1978, 26, 81–91.

Segal, S. J. *Imagery: Current Cognitive Approaches*. New York: Academia, 1971.

Sheehan, D. V.; Latta, W. D.; Regina, E. G.; and Smith, G. M. Empirical assessment of Spiegel's Hypnotic Induction Profile and eye-roll hypothesis. *IJCEH*, 1979, 28, 103–110.

Shor, R. E. Hypnosis and the concept of the generalized reality-orientation. *AJP*, 1959, 13, 582–602.

———, and Orne, M. T. *Harvard Group Scale of Hypnotic Susceptibility*. Palo Alto, Calif.: Consulting Psychologists Press, 1962.

———, and Orne, M. T. Norms on the Harvard Group Scale of Hypnotic Susceptibility, form A. *IJCEH*, 1963, 11, 39–47.

———, and Orne, M. T. *The Nature of Hypnosis*. New York: Holt, Rinehart, and Winston, 1965.

Slotnick, R. S.; Liebert, R. M.; and Hilgard, E. R. The enhancement of muscular performance in hypnosis through exhortation and involving instructions. *Journal of Personality*, 1965, 33, 37–45.

———, and London, P. Influence of instructions on hypnotic and non-hypnotic performance. *JAP*, 1965, 70, 38–46.

Spiegel, H. A single-treatment method to stop smoking using ancillary self-hypnosis. *IJCEH*, 1970, 18, 235–250.

———. The grade 5 syndrome: The highly hypnotizable

person. *IJCEH*, 1974, 22, 303–319.

———, and Bridger, A. A. *Manual for the Hypnotic Induction Profile: Eye-roll Levitation Technique*. New York: Soni Medica, 1970.

———, and Spiegel, D. *Trance and Treatment: Clinical Uses of Hypnosis*. New York: Basic Books, 1978.

Stoker, Bram. *Dracula*. New York: Airmont, 1965.

Tellegen, A., and Atkinson, G. Openness to absorbing and self-altering experiences (absorption), a trait related to hypnotic susceptibility. *JAP*, 1974, 83, 268–277.

Thomas, Lewis. *Late Night Thoughts on Listening to Mahler's Ninth Symphony*. New York: Viking Press, 1983.

Warner, K. E. The use of hypnosis in the defense of criminal cases. *IJCEH*, 1979, 27, 417–436.

Warren, Robert Penn. *All the King's Men*. New York: Bantam, 1963.

Weitzenhoffer, A. M. *Hypnotism: An Objective Study in Suggestibility*. New York: Wiley, 1953.

———. *General Techniques of Hypnosis*. New York: Grune and Stratton, 1957.

———; Gough, P. B.; and Landes, J. A study of the Braid effect: Hypnosis by visual fixation. *JP*, 1959, 47, 67–80.

———, and Hilgard, E. R. *Stanford Hypnotic Susceptibility Scale, form C*. Palo Alto, Calif.: Consulting Psychologists Press, 1962.

———, and Hilgard, E. R. *Stanford Profile Scales of Hypnotic Susceptibility: forms I and II*. Palo Alto, Calif.:

Consulting Psychologists Press, 1963.

———, and Sjoberg, B. M. Suggestibility with and without "induction of hypnosis." *JNMD*, 1961, 132, 204–220.

Wester, W. C., and Smith, A. H. Jr. (eds.). *Clinical Hypnosis: A Multidisciplinary Approach*. Philadelphia: Lippincott, 1984.

Wolpe, J. *Psychotherapy by Reciprocal Inhibition*. Stanford: Stanford University Press, 1958.

Worthington, T. S. The use in court of hypnotically enhanced testimony. *IJCEH*, 1979, 27, 402–416.

Young, P. C. Anti-social uses of hypnosis. In L. M. LeCreon (ed.), *Experimental Hypnosis*. New York: Macmillan, 1952.

Index